HOTEL  SIMULATION and AUDITING MANUAL

HOTEL OPERATIONS SIMULATION and AUDITING MANUAL

Patrick J. Moreo
Oklahoma State University

Gail Sammons
University of Nevada, Las Vegas

Cihan Cobanoglu
University of Delaware

Upper Saddle River, New Jersey 07458

Library of Congress Cataloging-in-Publication Data

Moreo, Patrick J.
  Hotel operations simulation and auditing manual / Patrick J. Moreo.-- 1st
ed.
     p. cm.
  Includes bibliographical references.
  ISBN 0-13-170461-3
  1. Hotels--Accounting. I. Title.
  HF5686.H75M674 2007
  657'.8374045--dc22   2005035399

Director of Development: Vernon R. Anthony
Senior Editor: Eileen McClay
Editorial Assistant: Marion Gottlieb
Executive Marketing Manager: Ryan DeGrote
Senior Marketing Coordinator: Elizabeth Farrell
Marketing Assistant: Les Roberts
Director of Manufacturing and Production:
   Bruce Johnson
Managing Editor: Mary Carnis
Production Liaison: Jane Bonnell

Production Editor: John Shannon/Laserwords
Manufacturing Manager: Ilene Sanford
Manufacturing Buyer: Cathleen Petersen
Senior Design Coordinator: Miguel Ortiz
Cover Designer: Marianne Frasco
Cover Image: Rob Brimson, Getty Images/Taxi
Composition: Laserwords Private Limited
Manager of Media Production: Amy Peltier
Media Production Project Manager: Lisa Rinaldi
Printer/Binder: Command Web

Pearson Prentice Hall™ is a trademark of Pearson Education, Inc.
Pearson® is a registered trademark of Pearson plc
Prentice Hall® is a registered trademark of Pearson Education, Inc.

Pearson Education LTD.
Pearson Education Singapore, Pte. Ltd.
Pearson Education Canada, Ltd.
Pearson Education—Japan
Pearson Education Australia PTY, Limited
Pearson Education North Asia Ltd.
Pearson Educación de Mexico, S.A. de C.V.
Pearson Education Malaysia, Pte. Ltd.

10 9 8 7 6 5 4 3 2 1
ISBN 0-13-170461-3

Contents

Introduction

The goals of *Hotel Operations Simulation and Auditing Manual* have evolved over the years. The manual still contains exercises to provide the user with a clearer insight into front office and guest accounting and operations. We accomplish this by having the student begin by performing a simple, manual audit of the guest accounts receivable, and then conclude with a computerized version of accomplishing the same thing in the *Micros Fidelio Opera* system. In the last edition (called *Front Office Operations and Auditing Workbook, second edition*), we added a section on operational auditing for front office and for guest services. This was to help provide tools for constant quality management and guest services. In this latest version, we have added another part to this operational auditing section on Housekeeping. Thus the concept of auditing is taken beyond the traditional auditing of guest accounts and extended to auditing the process and quality of the operations necessary to create the guest experience.

While there are some hotels and inns which continue to use a hand transcript, the purpose here is not to necessarily teach the student "how to" perform the manual night audit. Rather, we hope that the insight gained by seeing all the components of the night audit laid out before them would provide the users with the basic tools necessary to transfer their understanding to the many computer systems which have been and will be developed for performing the front office guest management accounting functions. These systems all change very rapidly in technical respects, but the underlying theories and principles remain the same: an audit and reconciliation of guests' bills with pertinent hotel records through standard bookkeeping and accounting techniques and the ability to track guest and room information with integration and ease.

In the first section, the student actually performs an entire day's front office transactions before beginning the audit itself. The preliminary front office guest management part of the exercise should put front office accounting operations into cycled perspective. For this reason, we strongly urge the student to complete the problem exercise in the order which the components of that problem appear – as though they were working in the front office from the morning on through the day and evening shifts and finally ending with the night audit itself.

The *Micros Fidelio* simulation section of this book is designed to illustrate how front office operations flow from the manual foundation, which we have laid in the context of an actual property management system. The goal is for the student to understand that regardless of the techniques used, ultimately it is a *system* design that will lead to the goal of providing the guest with excellent, quick service and the hotel with accurate records. The student should have a clear understanding that indeed, with evolving computer driven systems, many of the checks and balances in the original manual system become unnecessary because the possibility for posting error, for example, is eliminated and because information need be entered into the system only once. *Hotel Operations Simulation and Auditing Manual* reinforces *theory* with practice.

The section on front office and housekeeping operational auditing can serve many purposes. At a minimum it aids students in getting an overview of how the many functions in the front office, which they read about in their textbook, are actually applied and evaluated. Students can make even more extensive use of this section by using the Operational Audit or parts of it on field visits to hotels as a guide to understanding the hotel or even as a basis for doing a project in a hotel. It lends itself particularly well to group projects.

Preface

This *Hotel Operations Simulation and Auditing Manual* is the result of experimentation in hotel operations and front office operations classes at the University of Nevada, Las Vegas, The Pennsylvania State University, New Mexico State University, Oklahoma State University, and the University of Delaware. It has evolved for over twenty years in providing a technique for students to get a practical understanding of what they are learning in class. The exercises are intended as reinforcement for the guest/room management as well as the accounting sections of lectures and textbooks in front office or hotel operations courses. The operational auditing section provides both a field experience guide for students and a generic quality audit for hotel operators.

Hotel Operations Simulation and Auditing Manual is especially designed to be compatible with the corresponding sections of the major hotel operations and front office texts in use. It will reinforce those sections of the texts dealing with guest and room status management and accounting with practical exercises.

The concept of using a practice set to reinforce classroom instruction is not new. As students at the New York City College of Technology (CUNY) in the mid-1960s, we used similar approaches under the direction of Professor Sam Iseman. I would like to remember the late Sam Iseman for his dedication and inspiration for this twenty-first century version.

This newly named manual evolved from the second Prentice Hall edition (fifth historical edition) with further innovation. We are very happy to welcome Dr. Cihan Cobanoglu and his computer exercise and tutorial addition to the *Manual*. Dr. Cobanoglu is a faculty member in Hotel and Restaurant Administration at the University of Delaware, specializing in hospitality technology. He has combined years of hospitality experience with a keen knowledge of I.T. The authors are grateful to Micros Fidelio for its cooperation in making the Opera system software available to Dr. Cobanoglu for use in this *Manual*. Students now have in these exercises access to one of the most popular and accessible property management systems on the market.

Dr. Gail Sammons has rewritten, refreshed, and updated the Sample Night Audit Exercise and the Problem Set that is included in this book. We have left these "hand done" manual night audit exercises in the book at the request of several users who see them as an excellent basis for understanding the management system underlying any computer platform of a property management system.

Finally, we have expanded the operational auditing section of the book. We have used recently completed research to add a Housekeeping Operational Audit to this section in addition to the Front Office Operational Audit, both of which can be used as a teaching/learning tool as well as a practical management tool in hotels. I received comments and suggestions from other instructors who have used this book and incorporated them into this edition. Please continue to communicate them to any of us.

Patrick J. Moreo, Ed.D., CHA
Stillwater, Oklahoma

Notes to Instructors

- Enough forms are included for one problem set. These forms may be copied.

- We have found it quite beneficial to change one or two numbers for each class so that some of the final figures will be different from semester to semester. This is relatively simple to do especially if you change those figures that will not affect the cash totals. If you contact the authors, we can provide you with further details on implementing this system with a minimum of effort.

- Also available is a diskette for instructors that has the solution sets on it and that can also be used to generate differences in the problem sets. This helps in making certain that each semester and each section is challenged with problem sets that are uniquely theirs.

- You can request hard copy solution sets or diskettes by contacting your Prentice Hall representative. Or you may contact any us directly for information:

Dr. Patrick J. Moreo
School of Hotel and Restaurant Administration
210 HESW
Oklahoma State University
Stillwater, OK 74074   Office phone: 405-744-8484
pmoreo@okstate.edu

Dr. Gail Sammons
William F. Harrah College of Hotel Administration
University of Nevada, Las Vegas
4505 Maryland Parkway, Box 456021
Las Vegas, NV 89154-6021   Office phone: 702-895-4462
gail.sammons@unlv.edu

Dr. Cihan Cobanoglu
Assistant Professor
Hotel, Restaurant, and Institutional Management
University of Delaware
14 W. Main St. Raub Hall
Newark, DE 19716   Office phone: 302-831-4881
cihan@udel.edu

HOTEL OPERATIONS SIMULATION and AUDITING MANUAL

Section 1
Learning Hotel Operations

After reading the appropriate chapters in the textbook you are using, this manual will provide you with some exercises that will help to illustrate and reinforce what you learned from the book and from your classroom experiences. First, you will have the opportunity to do a "manual" night audit to experience the aspects of front office accounting. Then you will have the opportunity to do a completely computerized property management simulation, reaching the similar conclusion that you did in the manual system. And finally, you will have the opportunity to use one or both of the operational audit sections to help you do a field trip to a hotel for an interview or an observation session or even later as an aid for an internship.

Guidelines for Students on the Night Audit

The first part of this section is designed to help you to understand the basics of designing and operating a system of guest accounts receivable and guest status management in the front office of a hotel or other lodging facility. It has been our experience and our belief, after teaching hundreds of students and conducting discussions with alumni in the years after they have graduated, that an understanding of the "manual" system is crucial to the comprehension of other systems.

Use of this manual system will make it very easy for you to see each component of the front office accounting and guest management system and how that component is interrelated to all the other parts of the system. This is because you will actually be manipulating each of these parts yourself.

Next, with this basic understanding, future application of the knowledge gained makes a lot more sense. So, when you begin to learn about the plethora of computer systems, you will know what these systems are supposed to do – because you have done it yourself!

Indeed, you will then to be able to clearly see what it is you would like the computer pro-grams to do, and what is no longer necessary compared to the manual or electronic systems. The perfect follow-up to performing these manual exercises is to do the same thing using a computer front office or property management system such as Micros Fidelio, M.S.I., H.I.S., Lodgistix or any of the other number of fine software packages or proprietary systems available either on your next job position or in a computer laboratory you might have available in your school. Computer systems will continue to rapidly change over the years. The practice and understand-ing you will receive in these exercises is an excellent preparation for the development and change that we will continue to see.

To help with this understanding and development, we have included a "computerized" section in this workbook. The disc and instructions will illustrate several things. First, what does the "environment" of a property management system look like? Reservations, registration, room availability display, folios and guest tracking and communications are greatly automated and simplified. Secondly, what does computer design mean for us in operating the hotel? An entry generally needs to be made only one time. Mistakes are much less frequent because we are not manually copying information from one place to another. Posting can be done from the point of sale in the hotel. And finally, each guest's information is available to many critical places on the property simultaneously. So, the front office, housekeeping, sales and catering, reservations and telecommunications, service staff, room service, and restaurants can all have the same live access. Transactions are greatly speeded up, and accuracy is increased.

But probably one of the most important things you should realize as you walk through the computerized example set is what it means for management. As guest service agents, supervisors, department heads, and managers, we are no longer bound by availability of equipment and information in one place. A service agent does not have to go to a particular file in the front office. Restaurants no longer have to wait on a phone to check to see if someone is registered and authorized to make a charge. Information is available simultaneously throughout the property. Thus, jobs themselves can be designed in very different ways. Each computer terminal provides everything we need to provide guest service, information, and accounting. Consider this as you are doing the computer exercise.

Please be sure to do the problems in the same order they would be done during the hotel workday. In the manual problems, don't try to do the transcript first, for example. Get the check-ins, the folios and the voucher posting done first. If you do, you'll have a much better understanding of what's going on and the problems will be more fun and less time consuming to do.

The Night Audit of Accounts Receivable

The purposes of performing the night audit include the following:

1. Ensure each guest account is correct

2. Ensure charges and credits have been properly posted for accounting purposes

3. Provide succinct and valuable management reports summarizing the salient features of the day's business.

The methods used to fulfill these purposes are varied, but might be summarized into three major categories for the sake of simplicity.

1. **Manual methods or the hand transcript** – very few of only the smallest lodging properties continue to use the hand transcript in practice. But, there are still some! Understanding the manual methods is still the key to understanding any other system that has evolved, especially computer property management systems. The manual system forces you to proceed through the system and look at each entry

separately. Much of what the software in the computer does is based on what happened in previous manual systems.

2. **Electronic methods,** – includes the use of posting machines (e.g. Micros, NCR, etc.) Most of these systems generally required the maintenance of paper folios to be used with limited machine memory. They have been almost completely phased out, but remain important in understanding historically the development of computer property management systems.

3. **Computer methods,** – including both PC (personal computer) driven systems and mainframe systems.

    a. PCs generally constitute small-scale computer systems, quite often integrating all front office functions including reservations and room status as well as the accounting functions for guests' accounts receivable. Depending on the size of the property and design of the system, the PC can operate as a stand-alone computer or integrated on a local area network (LAN).

    b. Full-scale, mainframe computer systems generally consist of a hotelwide system including many terminals and driven from one large central processing unit. The scope and use of these "mainframe" systems are rapidly changing as the individual PCs and LANs become extremely powerful.

In the past, the PC and the mainframe have been two very distinct types of computer systems. The last few years have seen tremendous advances in technology. These advances continue and in so doing allow small properties to begin with systems of the appropriate size and complexity for the property's small size, but with the ability to expand both software and hardware with growth in both size and computer sophistication.

The concept of "networking" PCs together has virtually made the possibility of computer use desirable in almost any size or type of property. Nevertheless, an understanding of the basic concepts as they are put forth in the manual system is crucial to making these evolving applications.

Finally, be prepared for many different applications in the field. Although most hotel and lodging properties are at least partially computerized, there are still a few especially smaller ones that are not. The principles of accuracy of guest bills, proper distribution of charges among operating departments, and availability of succinct management reports remain the same. Executing them becomes more efficient, faster, and simpler as computer applications become more sophisticated.

In any case, the following formula summarizes the requirements for the night audit to be satisfactorily completed regardless of which system is used.

The Night Audit Formula

The Calculation	The Proof
TODAY'S OPENING GUEST LEDGER BALANCE (from folios)	(Must equal yesterday's closing balance.)
+ TODAY'S CHARGES (from folios)	(Must equal today's voucher totals for each department, which must equal departmental control totals for each department.)
– TODAY'S CREDITS (from folios)	(Must equal today's voucher totals for each department, or cash, or transfers as appropriate and must equal any departmental control totals as appropriate.)
= TODAY'S CLOSING GUEST LEDGER BALANCE	(Must equal the total of the folio closing balances on folio balance sheet, tape, or total.)

Immediately following the directions for student use, there is a sample job analysis for the manual night audit. It is included as a guideline in arriving at a management perspective concerning the night audit. It should serve as a reminder that similar outlines should be prepared for the night audit (or any front office job), regardless of what system is used to perform the audit. The analysis is a training aid and provides a measure of security for the new employee, especially on the first few shifts they work by themselves.

To be sure, the analysis included here is simply a sample. Most hotels have their own particular way of doing things. Yet, the basic procedures are undoubtedly common to all lodging facilities. Certainly, management could take the analysis further, fleshing it out to a full-scale procedural manual by explaining each job analysis step in more detail and illustrating the steps with sample calculations, diagrams, forms, and photographs.

In front office systems using electronic posting machines or computers, clearly labeled diagrams and photographs should illustrate the function and position of each key, switch or screen in the proper order. This is primarily for the benefit of employees who are not familiar with the system and so should be as simply and clearly stated as possible.

Most contemporary computer software should include optional "help" instructions directly in the program sequence, thus making it as user friendly as possible. By making the help screens optional, they are available when needed but not necessary to the function of the program, and thus do not slow down the seasoned user. More powerful graphics and expanded memory also make it possible for screen displays to be very illustrative and self-explanatory. The more closely the screen can resemble the configuration of the hotel or the guest bill itself, for example, the simpler it will be for associates to train on and use.

Finally, the analysis for the manual night audit should serve as an aid to the student who is going to complete the problem set contained herein in conjunction with classroom lectures and any accompanying textbook and the completed sample night audit forms that follow the analysis.

Section 2
Manual Night Audit Exercise

Directions for the Student Exercise

Hotel Operations Simulation and Auditing Manual actually encapsulates the entire hotel day's work in the front office including check-ins, checkouts, postings, and other transactions. You actually perform an entire day's front office transactions before beginning the audit itself. The preliminary front office guest management part of the exercise should put front office accounting operations into cycled perspective. For this reason, we strongly urge you to complete each problem in the order in which the components of that problem appear – as though you were working in the front office from the morning on through the day and evening shifts and finally ending with the night audit itself.

So for you to realize the full benefit of the exercise, it is best to approach it as realistically as possible. This means that the transactions should be made in roughly the same order in which they would chronologically happen. Thus, all the check-ins, checkouts, postings and other trans-actions should be completed prior to beginning the night audit procedure itself. You should refer to whichever main text or handouts you are using for the course as a guide for guest registration, folio preparation, etc.

In other words, you will, for the first part of the exercise, do the work of the day and swing shift receptionist and cashiers. You will then begin the work of the night auditor. At that point it would be beneficial to begin to use the sample "Job Analysis" as an instructional guide.

Sample Job Analysis for Manual Night Audit

1. Read logbook and any new memos or communications.

2. Obtain any necessary information from the off-going shift.

3. Count cash (if using common bank with other shifts).

4. Post any charges that still remain from the previous shift.

5. Prepare the Room and House Count Report (if not done by a night clerk).

6. Total charge and credit vouchers by department, fastening an adding machine tape to each packet of vouchers.

7. Check voucher packet totals against departmental control sheet totals if available.

8. Post room and tax to each folio.

9. Add total charges, total credits and closing balance for each folio.

10. Post the charges and credits from each folio to the transcript sheet.

11. When all folios are posted to the transcript, add the total charges, the total credits, and the closing balance for each room entered on the transcript.

12. Foot and cross-foot the transcript (add rows across and columns down). This simply ensures that there are no mathematical errors; it does not mean the audit is in balance.

13. Verify that the departmental total columns on the transcript agree with the voucher totals (and with the departmental control sheet totals) for each department.

14. Make an adding machine tape that includes the closing balance of each guest ledger folio. The total of the tape is the guest ledger closing balance for today.

15. Verify that the total guest ledger balance for today according to the adding machine tape of the folio closing balances agrees with the total, net guest ledger closing balance as shown on the transcript. The night audit is in balance if the totals indicated to this point agree.

16. Carry forward the closing balance for each room on today's transcript as the opening balance on tomorrow's transcript.

Sample Night Audit Exercise for the University Inn

Introduction

- This exercise is an example of performing the night audit.

- Included at the end of the exercise are the completed cash sheet, cash envelope, room and house count sheet, and the transcript sheet.

- Brief notes appear on these completed forms to help you understand how each document ties together. Of course you shouldn't write these notes on your forms when you do the subsequent problems.

Sample Exercise

Following are the guest ledger balances at the close of the night audit for April 24. They become the opening balances for April 25, 20___.

Room #	Guest Names	# of Guests	Room Rate	Opening Balance for April 25, 20___
202	Mr. Rocky Roach	1	$50.00	$63.48
207	Mr. and Mrs. Phil Up	2	50.00	12.25
208	Mr. Drew Down	1	75.00	156.04
210	Mr. Stan Ipslinski	1	50.00	74.00

The following are the summaries of the departmental control sheets and other transactions for April 25, 20___.

1. Mr. Roach pays his account with cash and checks out. (After his charge is posted.)

2. Mr. Down in 208 pays $150.00 on account and will stay another night. His room rents for $75.00.

3. Mr. and Mrs. Francisco Ramos and child of No. 20 Forbes Park, Manila, Philippines check in to Room 201 at $100.00 per night. They will stay three nights.

4. Mr. Leonardo Da Vinci checks in to Room 204. He had an advance deposit in the City Ledger of $75.00. He will stay two nights and is from 500 Broadway, New York, NY 10001. The room rate is $75.00.

5. Mr. and Mrs. Ramos in Room 201 have a tip paid-out to the restaurant for $2.50.

6. Ms. Sadie Silver and Ms. Nelly Nod check in to Room 206. The total room rate is $84.00. They are with the Kold Kreem Company of 1 Main Street, Union City, NJ 10033. They will stay one night.

7. Rabbi Jacob Josephson checks in to Room 209 for one week at the daily rate of $48.00. He is from 25 Park Place, New York, NY 10002.

8. Mr. Ipslinski in Room 210 complains to the assistant manager that his shirt was not folded as he had requested, but was placed on a hanger instead. The assistant manager authorizes an allowance of $5.00 off his laundry charge from April 24.

9. Mr. Ipslinski, in Room 210, pays his account with an American Express credit card and checks out. (There are no further charges.)

10. Mr. and Mrs. Conrad Vanderbuilt check in to Room 210 for one week at the daily rate of $90.00 per day. They have a $90.00 advance deposit in the City Ledger and reside at 201 Magnolia Lane, Oil City, TX 92543.

11. A C.O.D. package arrives for Mr. Vanderbuilt (Room 210) for which the cashier makes a $5.72 paid-out to the postman.

12. Mr. and Mrs. Up (Room 207) have requested that $16.40 of Mr. Down's bill be transferred to their account.

13. Mr. and Mrs. Up (Room 207) pay with traveler's checks after their charge is posted and check out.

14. Mr. and Mrs. Salvatore Fertilla and their five children check in to Rooms 202/203. The total rate is $150.00. They will stay for one night and are from 27 Lombard Street, San Francisco, CA 88552.

15. Flowers from the Daisy Flower Shop arrive for Mr. Vanderbuilt (Room 210) for which the cashier makes a paid-out for $30.50.

16. Mr. and Mrs. Fertilla (Rooms 202/203) pay $175.00 on account by personal check.

17. Ms. Silver (Room 206) pays $6.27 on account.

18. Mr. and Mrs. Pat Moreo and child, of the University of Nevada, Las Vegas, check in to Room 207. The room is a $40.00 special rate. They pay for two nights room and tax at check-in with an approved personal check.

Restaurant Summary April 25, 20—			Beverage Summary April 25, 20—		
201	(Ramos)	$15.00	201	(Ramos)	$7.50
202	(Roach)	$5.75	204	(Da Vinci)	$10.50
202/3	(Fertilla)	$27.00	208	(Down)	$9.50
202/3	(Fertilla)	$58.00	206	(Nod)	$6.50
206	(Silver)	$8.19	210	(Vanderbuilt)	$52.75
210	(Vanderbuilt)	$120.00	206	(Nod)	$9.01
209	(Josephson)	$8.75			

Local Telephone Summary April 25, 20__			Long-Distance Telephone Summary April 25, 20__		
204	(Da Vinci)	$2.00	202/3	(Fertilla)	$3.81
202/3	(Fertilla)	$3.00	206	(Silver)	$6.27
209	(Josephson)	$2.00	210	(Vanderbuilt)	$57.50
209	(Josephson)	$2.00	208	(Down)	$2.80
210	(Vanderbuilt)	$1.00	207	(Up)	$8.16
207	(Moreo)	$2.00	207	(Moreo)	$3.25

Notes:

1. Room tax is computed at 10%.

2. Blank folios have been provided for the rooms occupied on April 24. You need not be concerned with addresses for these guests if none are given. Assume that they already have registration cards on file.

3. The following are the contents of the cash drawer at the close of business. The drawer started with a $500.00 bank.

Personal Checks:	$175.00
	69.23
	88.00
Traveler's Checks:	$210.00
Currency:	$110.00
	90.00
	150.00
	38.00
Quarters:	$36.00
Dimes:	13.70
Nickels:	6.10
Pennies:	.56

9

Sample Night Audit Forms

Sample Night Audit Forms for the University Inn for this sample audit are shown on the following pages.

UNIVERSITY INN
FRONT OFFICE CASH SHEET
Sample Audit

Date: April 25, 20____

Cash Receipts   Disbursements—Guests

Room #	Name	Amount	Room #	Name	Item	Amount
202	Mr. Rocky Roach	$69.23	201	M/M Ramos	Tip/Rest	$2.50
208	Mr. Drew Down	150.00	210	Mr. C. Vanderbuilt	C.O.D.	5.72
207	M/M Phil Up	36.81	210	Mr. C. Vanderbuilt	Flowers	30.50
202/3	M/M S. Fertilla	175.00				
206	Ms. S. Silver	6.27				
207	M/M P. Moreo	88.00				
	Guest Disbursements Subtotal					38.72
	Cash Disbursements - House					
	House Disbursements Subtotal					0.00
			RECAPITULATION			
				Total Cash Receipts		**$525.31**
				Disbursements—Guests		38.72
			+	Disbursements—House		0.00
			−	Total Disbursements		38.72
Cash Receipts Total		**$525.31**	=	**Deposit**		**$486.59**

Agrees with Cash Disbursement on Transcript

Agrees with Column 17

Cash Receipts on the Daily Transcript

Agrees with Deposit on Cash Turn-In Envelope

UNIVERSITY INN
CLOSING BANK COUNT
Sample Audit

Cashier Name:	Gail Sammons
Cashier Shift:	Swing
Date:	April 25, 20__

Bills:	$100.00	
	50.00	
	20.00	110.00
	10.00	90.00
	5.00	150.00
	1.00	38.00
Coins:	.50	
	.25	36.00
	.10	13.70
	.05	6.10
	.01	0.56
	Subtotal	$444.36
	Due Back	$55.64
=	TOTAL BANK	$500.00

Agrees with Due Back on Cash Turn-In Envelope

Agrees with Due Back on Closing Bank Count Sheet

Agrees with Deposit on Front Office Cash Sheet

UNIVERSITY INN
CASH TURN-IN ENVELOPE
Sample Audit

Cashier Name:	Gail Sammons
Cashier Shift:	Swing
Date:	April 25, 20__

Bills:	$100.00	
	50.00	
	20.00	
	10.00	
	5.00	
	1.00	
Coins:	.50	
	.25	
	.10	
	.05	
	.01	

Checks and Vouchers

Personal Check	175.00
Personal Check	69.23
Personal Check	88.00
Traveler's Checks	210.00
Total Amount Enclosed	$542.23
– DUE BACK	$55.64
= DEPOSIT	$486.59
– DEPOSIT (from cash sheet)	$486.59
DIFFERENCE (over/short)	$0.00

This envelope is deposited in safe at the end of shift.

University Inn
Daily Transcript of Guest Ledger (Sample Audit)

April 25, 20

1 Folio No.	2 Room No.	3 No. of Guests	4 Opening Balance DB (CR)	5 Room Rate	6 Room Tax	7 Restaurant	8 Beverages	9 Local Calls	10 Long Distance	11 Laundry	12 Valet	13 Misc. Charges	14 Cash Disburse.	15 Transfer Debit	16 Total Daily Charges	17 Cash Receipts	18 Allowances	19 Transfer to City Ledger	20 Transfer Credit	21 Total Credits	22 Closing Balance
	201	3		100.00	10.00	15.00	7.50						2.50		135.00					0.00	135.00
	202	7		150.00	15.00	85.00		3.00	3.81						256.81	175.00				175.00	81.81
	203	See 202																			0.00
	204	1		75.00	7.50		10.50	2.00							95.00				75.00	75.00	20.00
	205																				0.00
	206	2		84.00	8.40	17.20	6.50		6.27						122.37	6.27				6.27	116.10
	207	3		40.00	4.00			2.00	3.25						49.25	88.00				88.00	-38.75
	208	1	156.04	75.00	7.50		9.50		2.80						94.80	150.00			16.40	166.40	84.44
	209	1		48.00	4.80	8.75		4.00							65.55					0.00	65.55
	210	2		90.00	9.00	120.00	52.75	1.00	57.50				36.22		366.47				90.00	90.00	276.47
Subtotal		20	156.04	662.00	66.20	245.95	86.75	12.00	73.63	0.00	0.00	0.00	38.72	0.00	1185.25	419.27	0.00	0.00	181.40	600.67	740.62
DEPARTURES																					
	202		63.48			5.75									5.75	69.23				69.23	0.00
	207		12.25						8.16					16.4	24.56	36.81				36.81	0.00
	210		74.00														5.00	69.00		74.00	0.00
Subtotal			149.73	0.00	0.00	5.75	0.00	0.00	8.16	0.00	0.00	0.00	0.00	16.40	30.31	106.04	5.00	69.00	0.00	180.04	0.00
GRAND TOTAL HOUSE			305.77	662.00	66.20	251.70	86.75	12.00	81.79	0.00	0.00	0.00	38.72	16.40	1215.56	525.31	5.00	69.00	181.40	780.71	740.62

Annotations:

- *Agrees with Total of all Current Folios added together*
- *Agrees with Voucher Totals for each column*
- *Agrees with Total Receipts from Cash Sheet*
- *Agrees with Guest Cash Disbursement from Cash Sheet*
- *Agrees with Voucher Totals*
- *Agrees with Voucher Totals for each Department AND with Departmental Control Sheets for Each Department*
- *Agrees with yesterday's Daily Balance*
- *Agrees with Room & House Count Sheet*

15

UNIVERSITY INN
ROOM AND HOUSE COUNT SHEET
Sample Audit

Date: April 25, 20___

Room Reconciliation

	No. of Rooms	No. of Persons	Room Value	Tax Value
Yesterday	4	5	$150.00	$15.00
+ Arrivals	8	19	587.00	58.7
= Total	12	24	737.00	73.7
– Departures	3	4	75.00	7.5
= Today	9	20	$662.00	$66.20

Agrees with totals for columns 3, 5, and 6, respectively, on transcript

Room Statistics

Rooms Available	10
Rooms Occupied	9
House Count	20
Average Rate per Occupied Room	$73.56
Average Rate per Guest	$33.10
Percentage of Occupancy	**90.0%**
Average Number of Guests per Room	2.2

Usually prepared from room rack.

Room #	No. of Guests	Room Rate	Tax
201	3	$100.00	$10.00
202/3	7	150.00	15.00
203	See Room 202		
204	1	75.00	7.50
205			
206	2	84.00	8.40
207	3	40.00	4.00
208	1	75.00	7.50
209	1	48.00	4.80
210	2	90.00	9.00
TOTAL	20.00	$662.00	$66.20

Agrees with totals for columns 3, 5, and 6, respectively, on transcript

Folio #: _____

UNIVERSITY INN
Sample Registration Card

Date April 25, 20__

Name **Francisco Ramos**
Street **No. 20 Forbes Park**
City **Manila** State **Philippines** Zip Code _____
Affiliation _____

Arrival Date	Room #	Rate	Clerk	Departure Date	Credit Card #
April 25, 20__	201	$100	GS	April 28, 20__	

Remarks: 2 adults, 1 child _____
_____
_____

Money, jewels, and other valuable packages must be placed in the safe in
the office. Otherwise the Management will not be responsible for any loss.

Cut along double lines   *Cut along double lines*

Folio #: _____

UNIVERSITY INN
Sample Registration Card

Date April 25, 20__

Name **Leonardo Da Vinci**
Street **500 Broadway**
City **NYC** State **NY** Zip Code **10001**
Affiliation _____

Arrival Date	Room #	Rate	Clerk	Departure Date	Credit Card #
April 25, 20__	204	$75	GS	April 27, 20__	

Remarks: Advance Deposit $75.00 _____
_____
_____

Money, jewels, and other valuable packages must be placed in the safe in
the office. Otherwise the Management will not be responsible for any loss.

No. 1001   **Sample Audit**   **Charge**

UNIVERSITY INN
Restaurant ___ Department

Date: ___ April 25, 20___ **209**

Name   Rabbi Jacob Josephson   Room or Acct. No.

Date	Symbol	Amount

Do not write in above space

EXPLANATION   Dinner $8.75

Signed by: *GS*

Cut along double lines.

No. 1003   **Sample Audit**   **Credit**

Transfer ___ Department

UNIVERSITY INN

Date: ___ April 25, 20___ **207**

Name   Mr. & Mrs. Phil Up   Room or Acct. No.

Date	Symbol	Amount

Do not write in above space

EXPLANATION   Transfer $16.40 from Mr. Down's (Room 208)   ($16.40)

Signed by: *GS*

No. 1002   **Sample Audit**   **Charge**

Cash Disbursement (Tip) ___ Department

UNIVERSITY INN

Date: ___ April 25, 20___ **201**

Name   Francisco Ramos   Room or Acct. No.

Date	Symbol	Amount

Do not write in above space

EXPLANATION   Paid out tip to K.T. in restaurant $2.50

Signed by: *GS*

Cut along double lines.

No. 1004   **Sample Audit**   **Credit**

Transfer ___ Department

UNIVERSITY INN

Date: ___ April 25, 20___ **204**

Name   Leonardo Da Vinci   Room or Acct. No.

Date	Symbol	Amount

Do not write in above space

EXPLANATION   Transfer advance deposit from City Ledger   ($75.00)

Signed by: *GS*

RESTAURANT DEPARTMENT CONTROL SHEET

NAME: __Sample Audit__   DATE: _April 25, 20___

VOUCHER #	ROOM NO.	GUEST NAME	AMOUNT	MEMO
	201	Ramos	$15.00	
	202	Roach	5.75	
	202/203	Fertilla	27.00	
	202/203	Fertilla	58.00	
	206	Silver	8.19	
	210	Vanderbuilt	120.00	
	206	Nod	9.01	
	209	Josephson	8.75	
Compares to Column #7 on				
Daily Transcript Sheet		**Total Amount**	**$251.70**	

BEVERAGE DEPARTMENT CONTROL SHEET

NAME: __Sample Audit__   DATE: _April 25, 20___

VOUCHER #	ROOM NO.	GUEST NAME	AMOUNT	MEMO
	201	Ramos	$7.50	
	204	Da Vinci	10.50	
	208	Down	9.50	
	206	Nod	6.50	
	210	Vanderbuilt	52.75	
Compares to Column #8 on				
Daily Transcript Sheet		**Total Amount**	**$86.75**	

UNIVERSITY INN

Sample Folio

Guest's Name: **Francisco Ramos** _____   Room #:   **201** _____

Departure Date: **April 28, 20__** _____   Today's Date: **April 25, 20__**

ALL ACCOUNTS ARE DUE WHEN RENDERED

DATE	April 25	April 26					
FORWARD	**$0.00**	**$135.00**					
Room	100.00						
Tax	10.00						
Restaurant	15.00						
Beverages	7.50						
Telephone—Local							
Telephone—L.D.							
Laundry							
Valet							
Misc. Charges							
Cash Disbursements	2.50						
Transfer Debits							
TOTAL DEBITS	**$135.00**						
Cash Received							
Allowances							
Transfer to City Ledger							
Transfer Credit							
TOTAL CREDITS	**$0.00**						
BALANCE FORWARD	**$135.00**						

UNIVERSITY INN
Sample Folio Bucket Balance Sheet

Date: **April 25, 20__**

This form takes the place of the calculator tape that would be run on folio balances. The final total of this tape should be equal to the total in column 22 on the daily transcript of the general ledger.

Room Number		Folio Closing Balance
201		$135.00
202		81.81
203		0.00
204		20.00
205		$0.00
206		116.10
207		(38.75)
208		84.44
209		65.55
210		276.47
Total		740.62

Night Audit Exercise for the University Inn

Introduction

- This exercise consists of performing the night audit using the hand transcript for the 10-room University Inn for the 13th of November, 20—.

- Please read this entire exercise before you begin completing any of the forms. Use only the information provided in this exercise, as the exercise is not related to the sample audit.

Exercise

Following are the guest ledger balances at the close of the night audit for November 13, 20—. *They become the opening balances for November 14, 20—.*

Room #	Guest Names	# of Guests	Room Rate	Opening Balance for November 14, 20—
201	Mr. and Mrs. F. Ramos	2	$100.00	$59.00
202/203	Mr. and Mrs. S. Fertilla	7		($17.79)
204	Mr. and Mrs. L. DaVinci	2	$75.00	$8.00
206	Mrs. S. Silver	1		$31.25
206	Mrs. N. Nod	1		$34.81
207	Mr. and Mrs. P. Moreo	3		($15.75) 11.75
208	Mr. D. Down	1		$21.84
209	Rabbi J. Josephson	1	$48.00	$29.55 20.80

Following are the transactions and summaries of the departmental charges for November 14.

1. Dr. and Mrs. John Rhodes check in to Room 205. Their address is UC Davis, CA 89623. The room rate is $117 per night. They had an advance deposit of $128.70. In addition, they pay another $250 in traveler's checks on account.

2. Mr. Down checks out of Room 208. He pays his account with traveler's checks.

3. The Fertilla family checks out of 202/203 with no further charges. Their credit balance must be returned to them.

29

4. Mr. and Mrs. Moreo check out of Room 207 (one night early). They ask that $8.75 which was charged to Josephson's account in Room 209 be transferred to their account first. They have a tip paid-out for $3. They pay their balance in cash.

5. Ms. Elaine Martucci of the Marine Midland Trust Co., Rochester, NY 14000, checks in to Room 203. The rate is $84 per night. She will pay with Visa.

6. Ms. Nod and Ms. Silver check out of Room 206. Nod pays her account with cash. Silver pays with Visa.

7. Dr. Rhodes has a miscellaneous paid-out for $7.25 for a fax sent to UC Davis.

8. Mr. Ramos in Room 201 has a C.O.D. delivery of theater tickets arrive, for which he has authorized a paid-out for $96.

9. Mr. Da Vinci checks out of Room 204. He pays his account with a Diner's Club card.

10. Mr. Richard Sullivan of 1701 Mission Vista drive, San Diego, CA 87524, checks in to Room 204. The rate is $60 per night. He will pay with an American Express card.

11. Mr. Sullivan of Room 204 has a tip paid-out for $2.50.

12. Mr. Vanderbuilt of Room 210 has a tip paid-out for $4.

13. Dr. Marie and Mr. Anthony Lucca of Temple University, Philadelphia, PA 12201, check-in to Room 208 at a nightly rate of $110. They had a advance reservation deposit of $121. They will pay the remainder of their account with Master Card.

14. Ms. Stephanie Baumweiss checks in to Room 202. Her address is Van Camps Publishing Co., McCormick Place, Chicago, IL 66220. She will stay a night and the room rate is $68. This will be a direct billing.

15. Mr. Oscar Lopez and Mr. George Whipple of Washington Publishing Co., 718 Broadway, N.Y.C., NY 10001, check-in to Room 207. They are unsure of how many nights they will stay. Mr. Lopez will pay with an American Express Card, and Mr. Whipple will pay with a Master Card. The room rate is $80 per night.

16. Mr. Lucca of Room 208 has a $7 tip paid-out.

17. Mr. Harvey Shade of 807 Main Street, Frisbee, OH 32221, checks in to Room 206 at a rate of $62 per night. He will stay two nights; he will pay in cash. He anticipates charges and so pays $200 on account.

18. Mr. Vanderbuilt asked to look at his account and tells us that he did not get through on one of the long distance calls for which he was billed yesterday. The assistant front office manager authorizes a Long Distance Telephone Adjustment of $4.80.

Restaurant Summary November 14, 20__			Beverage Summary November 14, 20__		
207	(Moreo)	$15.75	210	(Vanderbuilt)	$32.00
206	(Silver)	$4.50	201	(Ramos)	$4.25
201	(Ramos)	$18.75	207	(Lopez)	$7.00
204	(Da Vinci)	$6.50	203	(Martucci)	$27.75
204	(Sullivan)	$15.50	207	(Whipple)	$6.75
208	(Lucca)	$40.00			
210	(Vanderbuilt)	$178.00			
205	(Rhodes)	$68.00			

Local Telephone Summary November 14, 20__			Long Distance Telephone Summary November 14, 20__		
204	(Da Vinci)	$2.00	206	(Nod)	$6.78
204	(Sullivan)	$1.00	204	(Da Vinci)	$10.60
210	(Vanderbuilt)	$3.00	201	(Ramos)	$7.80
203	(Martucci)	$1.00	203	(Martucci)	$4.55
208	(Lucca)	$1.00			

Notes:

1. Create folios for the room occupied on November 13. You need not be concerned with addresses for these guests if none are given. Assume that they already have registration cards on file.

2. Room tax is computed at 10%.

3. The following are the contents of the cash drawer at the close of business. The drawer started with a $500.00 bank.

Personal Checks:	$250.00
	220.00
Traveler's Checks:	$220.00
Currency:	$40.00
	80.00
	30.00
	42.00
Quarters:	$12.25
Dimes:	5.20
Nickels:	3.55
Pennies:	.96

Section 3
Computer Property Management
Exercise and Tutorial

Introduction to *Micros/Fidelio Opera*

The *Micros/Fidelio Opera* simulation section of this book is designed to illustrate how front office operations flow from the manual foundation, which we have laid in the context of an actual property management system. The goal is for the student to understand that regardless of the techniques used, ultimately it is a *system* design that will lead to the goal of providing the guest with excellent, quick service and the hotel with accurate records. The student should have a clear understanding that indeed, with evolving computer-driven systems, many of the checks and balances in the original manual system become unnecessary because the possibility of posting error, for example, is eliminated and because information need be entered into the system only once.

Hotel Operations Simulation and Auditing Manual reinforces *theory* with practice. The exercises in the *Micros/Fidelio Opera* section are intended as reinforcement for the guest/room management as well as the accounting sections of lectures and textbooks in front office or hotel operations courses.

About Opera Hotel Edition

Opera Demo Installation, Version 2.0.45.33

Copyright © 2002 MICROS Systems, Inc.

Dear User,

Please read these instructions before you use the software that came with this book.

You have received three CDs with this book. These CDs include *Micros/Fidelio Opera Hotel Edition Demo Software (Opera)* and the e-learning (tutorial) portion. The first two CDs include the actual software for the program. The third CD includes the e-learning portion for the software. We advise that you familiarize yourself with the software by this e-learning CD first. *Micros/Fidelio Opera Hotel Edition* is a comprehensive software. Therefore it is important to review this document and the tutorials on the e-learning CD. Please note that this is a full working version of the software designed specifically for this book and educational use only. Using this software for any purpose other than educational will be violation of copyright laws.

These instructions are prepared for you to get the maximum benefit from the software within the context of this textbook.

First, let's look at the system requirements that you will need.

System and Environment Prerequisites and Requirements

You must have the following minimum operating specifications loaded on your machine prior to installation commencing.

Hardware: Pentium II PC300MHz or above with a CD drive; mouse or trackball pointing device; with the screen resolution set to 1024 × 768 and displaying 256 colors. Optimal appreciation of the application will be seen using a 17" monitor. To be able to print the forms and reports, you need to have a printer installed in your system.

Operating System: Windows NT 4.0 with Service Pack 6a or Windows 2000 with Service Pack 2. This demo system has not been tested in Windows XP environment by Micros. However, the authors installed this demo CD into an XP computer and ran the system without any problem. **Please remember that neither Micros nor Prentice Hall provides any kind of technical assistance for these demo programs.** Both of these environments were used during the demo evaluations. Other operating systems may be compatible; however, it is not recommended.

Software: For contract and Adobe Acrobat documents, your PC needs to have Microsoft Word, Excel, Adobe Acrobat Reader and Outlook.

RAM: 256 MB minimum.

Disk Storage: A full copy of Oracle 8i will be installed on your system with this demo. The demo will require 4.0 GB of hard disk storage space. We recommend using a dedicated PC for this demo, which must **NOT** already be running Oracle for any other purpose. An additional 2 GB of free space in the system\Temp folder is required for installation.

Network Card: Includes a valid Internet Protocol (IP) address.

Web Browser: Internet Explorer 5.1 or 5.5 Service Pack 2. The Java VM option (JAVA JIT Compiler) must be enabled. The Web browser is used to access the online documentation and the client.

Software: Adobe Acrobat Reader 4.0 or above. The Adobe Acrobat Reader is used to preview and print reports within the *Opera* application. This software can be downloaded from www.adobe.com.

Required Folders: Ensure that you have the folder **C:\TEMP.**

IMPORTANT NOTE: If your computer has or had Oracle products installed, then DO NOT install Opera in your computer.

Pearson Education does not support third-party software.

Installing the Opera Demo

Once you have made sure that the computer you are installing *Opera* on does/did not have any Oracle products installed, then you can start installing this product. The complete installation processes including all the Oracle, Application Server components, *Opera* Database, and Schemas will take approximately 1 to $1^1/_2$ hours to complete.

1. Boot your PC and sign on with Administrator privileges.

2. Insert disk #1 of the *Opera* Demo CD in the CD drive.

3. Double click the b45p33demo.exe to start the installation.

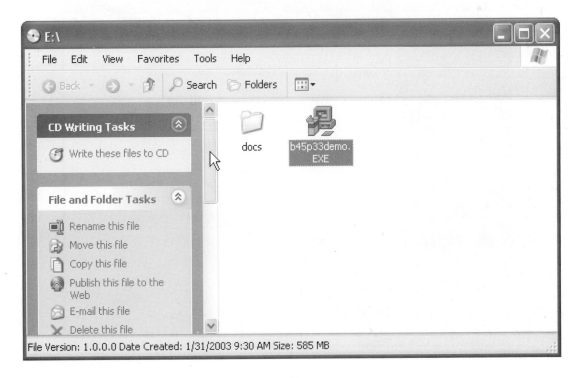

Step 1—Applications Server and Database Install

Select **Next.**

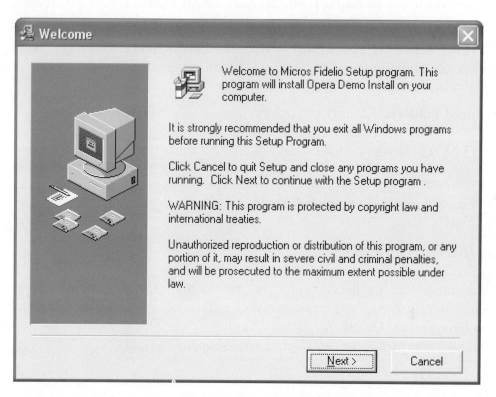

Select **Next.** Select a drive to install your *Opera* Demo. (Select a drive that has at least 4 GB space.)

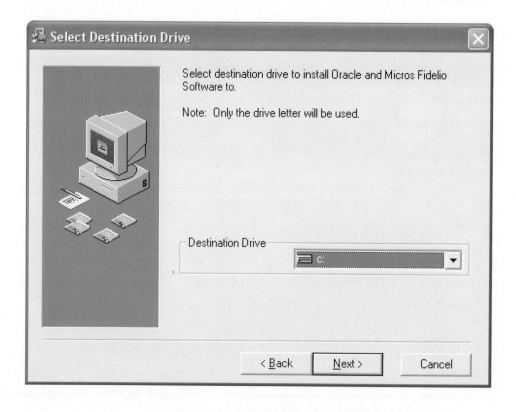

Select **Next** to start the install.

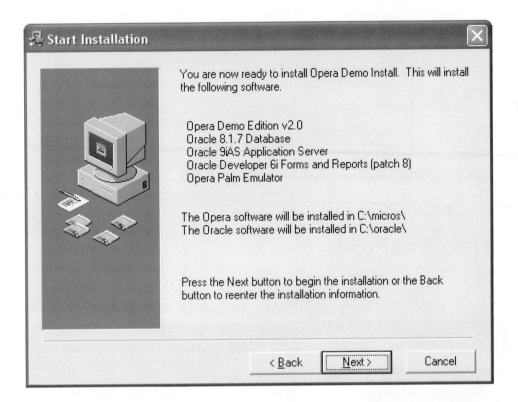

Files copying . . . no interaction needed.

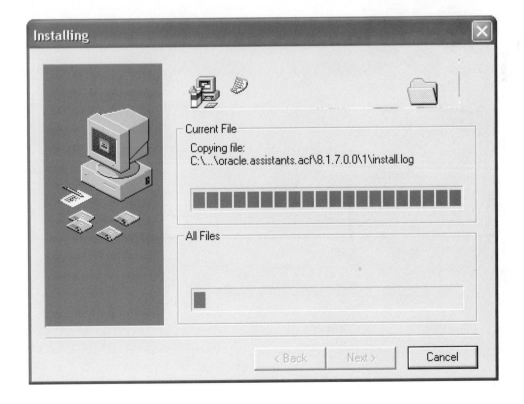

Insert disk #2 of the *Opera* Demo CD in the CD drive and press the OK button.

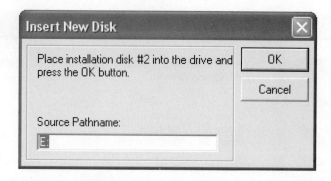

Files copying . . . no interaction needed.

The Install is complete. Select **Finish.**

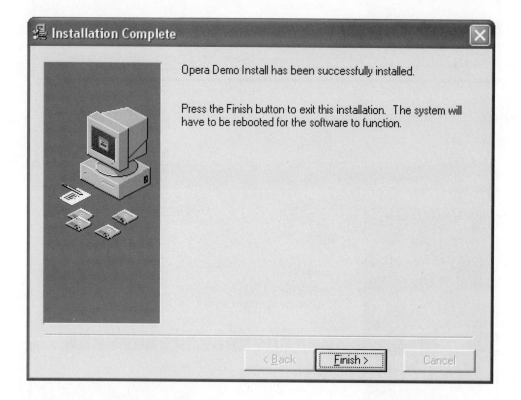

Step 2—Reboot the System

Please restart your computer.

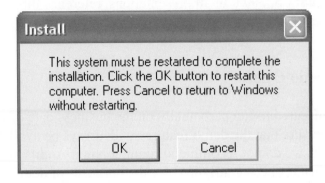

Now, *Opera* has been installed on your computer. Congratulations. You can now use your software. Before you actually use *Opera*, please make sure you are comfortable with the material in the tutorial CD that came with your book.

How to Run the Opera PMS

This section will assist users in navigating the **Opera Property Management System (PMS).** The program that came with your book is a full working copy of *Opera*; however, certain limitations are in place that limit the use of the demo. Specifically, hotels may have no more than 500 rooms. There is a 1,000-transaction limit on the number of financial postings supported by the demo database.

Please do not change the descriptive name of the hotels (as established by the **Name** field configured in Property Details), which must be

       Property 1   Opera Demo Multi Hotel

       Property 2   Opera Demo Multi Hotel

       Property 3   Opera Demo Multi Hotel

This demo has been configured to run perpetually on the business date of **February 03, 2003.** This is the only way to ensure that the presentation of the features following will always be available for demo purposes. Because of this, we do not recommend running Night Audits on this demo database, as it will alter the data that has been configured for the purposes of demonstrating the *Opera* product. These stipulations should in no way prevent you from experiencing all of *Opera*'s features.

To assist you in providing a meaningful Opera product demonstration, we have included a high-level demonstration format highlighting the main *Opera* modules as well as providing you with the data to retrieve when presenting *Opera*. Three properties are configured for your use.

Logging onto the Database

Please note the business date on all properties has been set to **February 3, 2003. Ensure your PC's date is set to February 3, 2003.** In all presentations, reference this date or beyond, as when creating a new reservation, for example.

Starting Micros/Fidelio Opera

This demo has been configured to run perpetually on the business date of February 3, 2003. This is the only way to ensure that the demo features will always be available for demo purposes. Because of this, we do not recommend running Night Audits on this demo database, as it will alter the data that has been configured for the purposes of demonstrating the *Opera* product. These stipulations should in no way prevent you from experiencing all of *Opera*'s features.

To change the date of your computer (for Windows 2000 and XP):

- Click on **Start.**

- Click on **Control Panel.**

- Click (or double click) on **Date and Time.**

- Change the date.

- Click **OK.**

Please note that even though this is a full working demo of *Opera* PMS, there are some limitations.

After you install **Micros/Fidelio Opera,** *you will see a set of icons and folders on your desktop. Before you start* **Opera,** *you need to set the date of your computer to February 3, 2003.*

Double click on **OperaDemo Shortcuts** folder to see the OperaDemo PMS icon. (See Figure 1.)

Figure 1: Opera and Oracle Icons

Click on **OperaDemo PMS** shortcut to start Opera program. (See Figure 2.)

Figure 2: OperaDemo Shortcuts

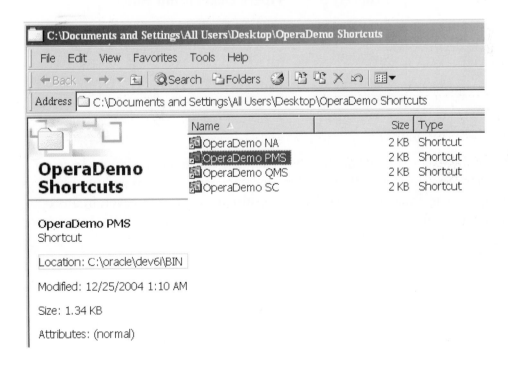

With this demo, you are given three different user names and passwords along with cashier IDs for three different properties.

The default log-on IDs and passwords are:

Property 1	**Opera Demo Multi Hotel**
User ID	OPERA1
Password	OPERADEMO
Cashier	1000

Property 2	**Opera Demo Multi Hotel**
User ID	OPERA2
Password	OPERADEMO
Cashier	1002

Property 3	**Opera Demo Multi Hotel**
User ID	OPERA3
Password	OPERADEMO
Cashier	1003

You will have to use one of these user name/password combinations to start *Opera*. Please note that with this demo, Property Management System, Sales and Catering System, and Quality Management System modules have been also activated. However, in this book, we will cover only the PMS functions. For this exercise, we have used the OPERA1 user name. You can see this login screen in Figure 3.

Figure 3: Login Screen for *Opera* Demo

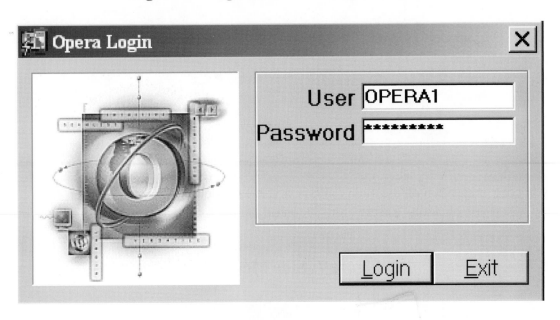

You will receive a message indicating the printer set-up. You can change this printer set-up from "Set-up." (See Figure 4.)

Figure 4:

In *Opera,* there are two sets of navigational toolbars. The first one is the horizontal main toolbar. (See Figure 5.)

Figure 5: Main Toolbar

If you click on the right arrow, you will see additional icons. (See Figure 6.)

Figure 6: The Additional Icons on the Main Toolbar

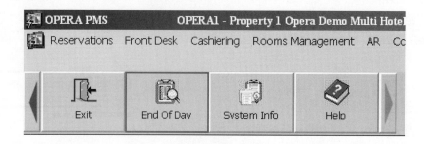

Once you click on an icon on the main toolbar, a vertical side menu bar will appear. For example, when you click on "Reservations" icon on the main toolbar (see Figure 7), you will see

Figure 7: Side Menu Bar

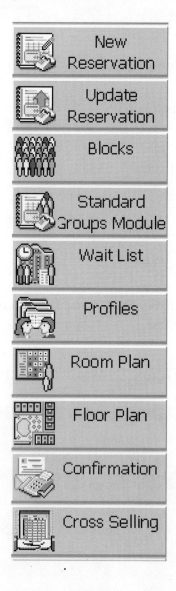

icons on the vertical side toolbar such as "New Reservation," "Update Reservation," and "Blocks." These side toolbars will change from icon to icon on the main toolbar.

Now, you have started *Opera*. The next step is to create a reservation.

Micros/Fidelio Opera Exercises

Creating a New Profile

In *Opera*, there is a concept of "Profiles," which allows guest records to be stored for a limited or unlimited time. A profile is a record of information. It consists of the main information about a guest, company, travel agent, group, or other source of a hotel reservation. A summary of future reservations and past stays is also included. Profiles are needed to create reservations in *Opera*. Even though there is a way to make a reservation without a profile, if the property wants to keep guest records for future use (i.e., yield management and customer relationship management), it is best to create a profile and then make a reservation. In profiles, *Opera* keeps all contact information, their preferences, account information, payment information including credit card numbers, memberships (i.e., Hotel Frequent Guest Program, Airline Frequent Miles Program), and rate information. All this information is then tied to reservations.

It is possible to create a profile for an individual, company, travel agent, group, or any other reservation source. In this exercise, we will create a profile for an individual.

Exercise: Creating a New Profile

Use the following information to create a profile in *Opera:*

First/Middle Name: John E.
Last Name: Korsek
Address: 14 W. Main St.
Newark, DE 19716 USA
Phone (302) 812-0090
Date of Birth: 09/09/1962
Interests: Special Promotions
Table game promotions
Mailings: New Year's mailing
Preferences: Local newspaper
Nonsmoking room
Ground floor

Suppose that your property (Opera1) has an agreement with American Airlines, and you give miles for stays. Mr. Korsek wants to include his AA Frequent Flyer Number in his profile. The information is as follows:

American Airlines Frequent Flyer Gold Member since 05/01/2001 with number 123456789. His membership will expire in 05/2005.

He also wants to keep his credit card number in file. His Visa card number is 4444 3333 2222 1111 with expiration date 05/2005. He will be given a "rack rate."

Let's do this by clicking on "Reservations" on the main toolbar (See Figure 8). Once the side toolbar appears, click on Profiles.

Figure 8: Profile Search Screen

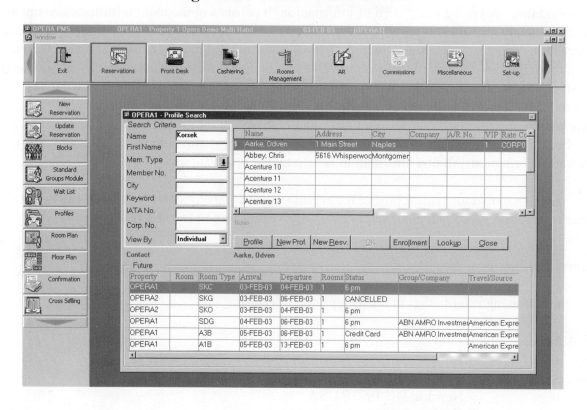

To create a new profile:

- Enter "Korsek" in the **Name** field as seen in Figure 8 and then press **Enter.**

- Because "Korsek" profile was not created before, it will not find it.

- Click on **New Prof.** to create a new profile for "Mr. Korsek."

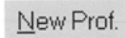

- Enter all contact information to the screen that follows. (See Figure 9.)

Figure 9: New Profile Screen

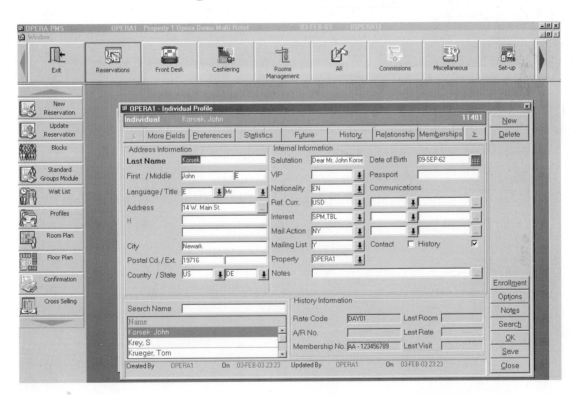

To enter the interests of the guest:

- Click on **Interest** on the main screen under **Internal Information.**

- You will see the screen in Figure 10.

- Click on **Special Promotions** and **Table Game Promotions.**

- You will see an **X** next to the selections.

- Press **OK.**

Figure 10: Interests Screen

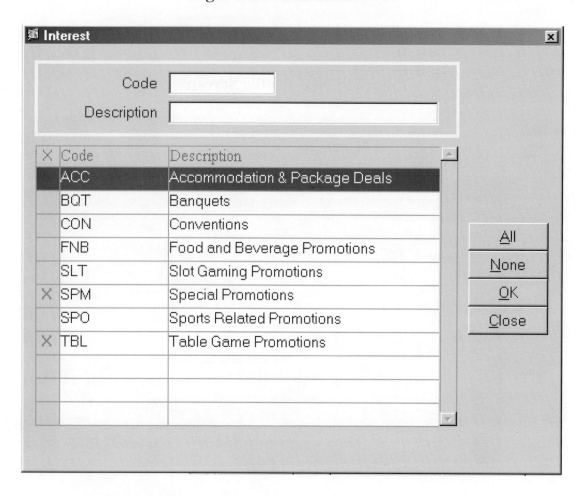

To include this guest for the mailing lists:

- Click on **Mail Action** on the main screen under **Internal Information.**

- Choose **New Year's Mailings** and then press **OK.** (See Figure 11.)

- Click on **Mailing List** and choose **Yes.**

Figure 11: Mailing List Screen

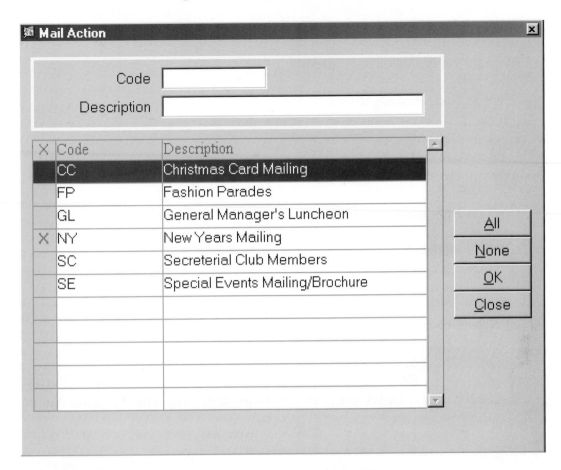

To record the preferences of Mr. Korsek:

- Click on **Preferences** tab.

- You will get the screen in Figure 12.

- Click on **New** to create a new preference.

- Click on **Newspaper.**

- You will get the screen in Figure 13.

- Click on **Local Newspaper.**

- Click on **OK.**

- You will be asked **Distribute preferences to other properties?** Answer **No.** (You should say **Yes** only if you have a chain hotel and you want this information to go to all other hotels within your chain.)

- Click on **New** again.

- Click on **Smoking.**

- You will get the screen in Figure 14.

- Click on **Non-smoking Room.**

- Click on **OK.**

- You will be asked **Distribute preferences to other properties?** Answer **No.**

- Click on **New** again.

- Click on **Floor.**

- You will get the screen in Figure 15.

- Click on **Ground Floor.**

- Click on **OK.**

- You will be asked **Distribute preferences to other properties?** Answer **No.**

Figure 12: Preferences Screen

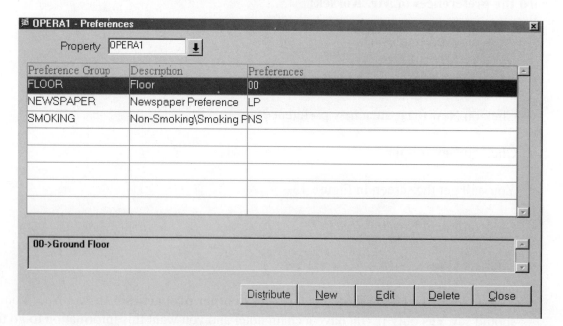

50

Figure 13: Newspaper Options in Preferences

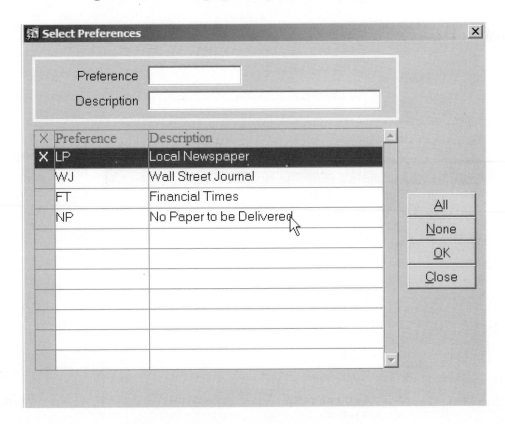

Figure 14: Smoking Preferences

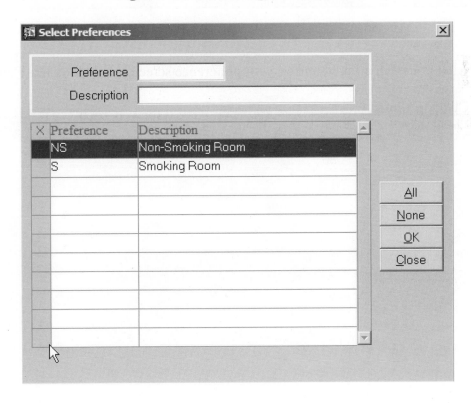

Figure 15: Floor Preferences

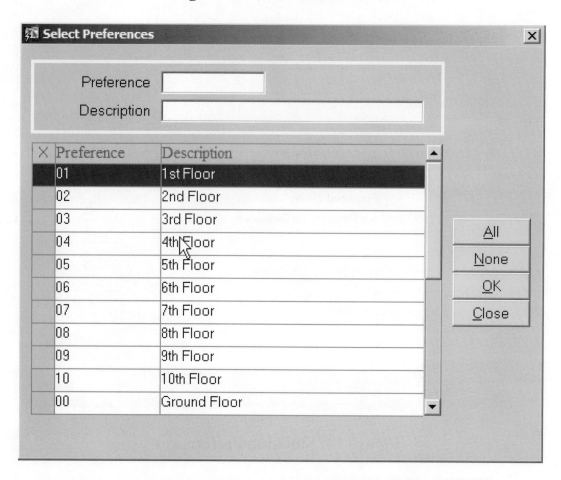

- After you enter all preferences, your preference screen should look like Figure 16.

- Click on **Close.**

52

Figure 16: The Preferences Screen after Selections

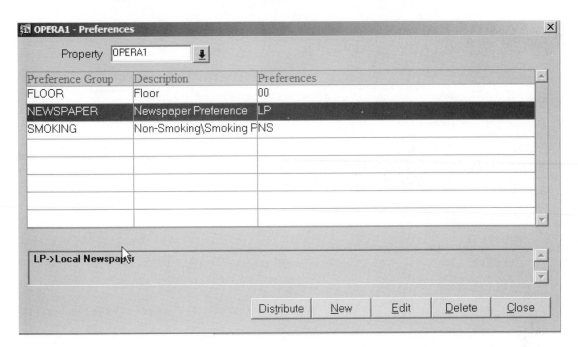

To enter American Airlines frequent flyer number to this profile:

- Click on **Membership** tab.

- Click on **New.**

- You will get the screen in Figure 17.

- Click on **Type** and choose **American Airlines.**

- Type the American Airlines Frequent Traveler number in **Card Number** box: 123456789.

- Click on **Expiration** box and enter 05/2005. (Note: Since your computer's date is in 2003, this expiration date will be good.)

- Click on **Joined Date** and enter 05/01/2001.

- Click on **OK.**

Figure 17: Membership Record Screen

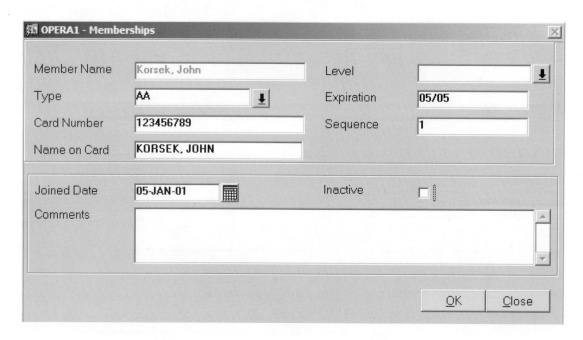

- After you enter all the information, your Membership screen should look like Figure 18.

- Click on **Close.**

Figure 18: Membership Screen

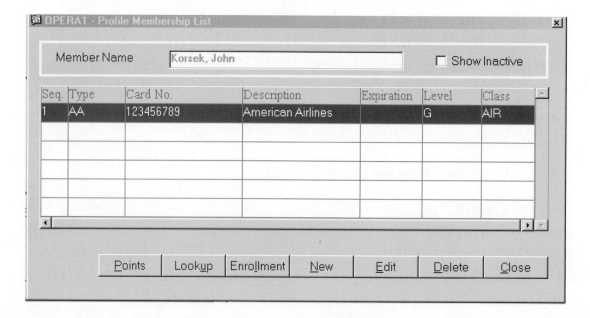

To enter a credit card to a profile:

- Click on **Credit Card** tab. (If you do not see **Credit Card** tab, you may need to click on right arrow to see it.)

- Click on **New.**

- You will see the screen in Figure 19.

- Click on **Type** and choose **Visa.**

- Click on **Credit Card Number** and type 4444333322221111 (spaces are not allowed).

- Click on **Expiration Date** and type 05/05. (Note: Since your computer's date is in 2003, this expiration date will be good.)

- Click on **Save.**

Figure 19: Credit Card Record Screen

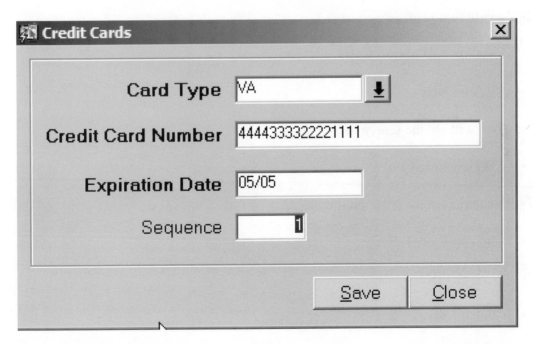

- After you enter credit card information, your credit card screen should look like Figure 20.

- Click on **Close.**

Figure 20: Credit Card List Screen

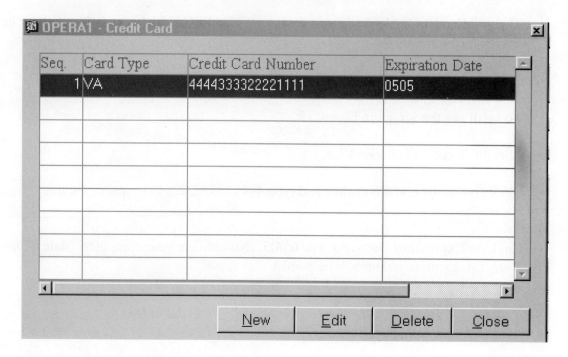

To assign a rate to a profile:

- Click on **Negotiated Rates.**

- Click on **New.**

- You will see the screen in Figure 21.

- Click on **Rate Code.**

- You will see the screen in Figure 22.

- Click on **Rack Rate.**

- Click on **OK.**

- Click on **Save.**

- You will be asked **Distribute Rate Code RACK to other properties?** Click on **No.**

- You will see the screen in Figure 23.

- Click on **Close.**

56

Figure 21: Negotiated Rates Screen

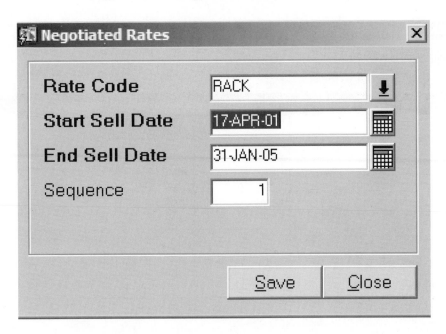

Figure 22: Rate Codes Screen

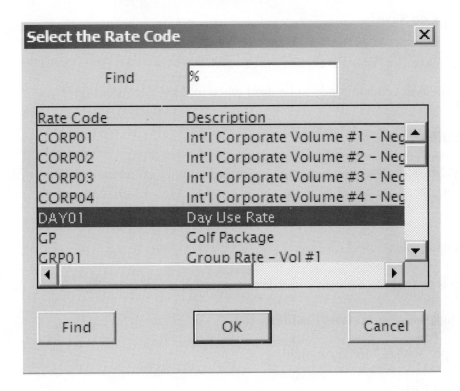

Figure 23: List of Negotiated Rates

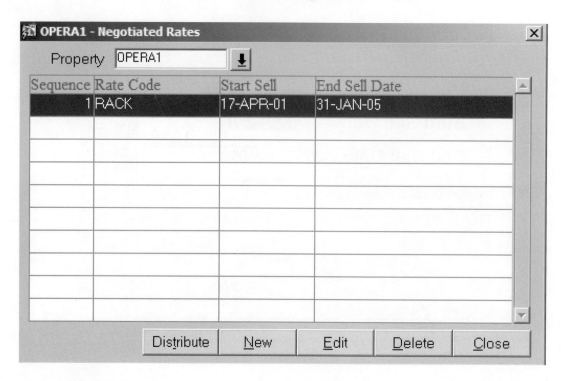

To save this profile:

- Click on **Save.**

- Click on **Close.**

Now, the profile is saved and ready to be used when making a reservation.

Exercise: Editing an Existing Profile

Let's say that Mr. Korsek called the hotel and added another credit card to his profile. This time, he gave you another Visa credit card with number 4444 3333 1234 1234 and expiration date of 05/2006.

Let's do this in *Opera*.

The first step is to find Mr. Korsek's profile among other existing profiles. To do this:

- Click on **Reservations/Profiles.**

- Type "Korsek" in **Name** field.

- Press **Enter.**

- You should see Mr. Korsek's profile in the screen as in Figure 24.

Figure 24: Mr. Korsek's Profile Information Screen

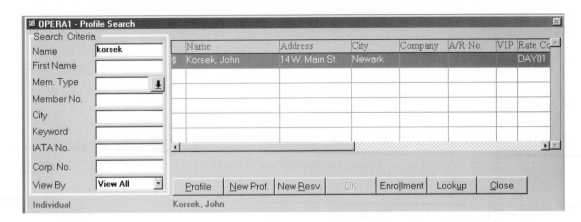

- Double click on Mr. Korsek's name in **Profiles** to edit it.

- Click on **Credit Card** tab.

- Click on **New.**

- You will see the screen in Figure 25.

- Click on **Type** and choose **Visa.**

- Click on **Credit Card Number** and type 4444333312341234 (spaces are not allowed).

- Click on **Expiration Date** and type 05/06.

- Click on **Save.**

- Click on **Close.**

Figure 25:

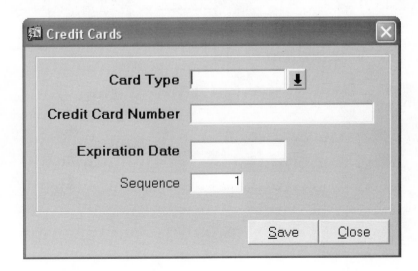

- You will come to main profiles screen.

- Click on **Save.**

- Click on **OK.**

Exercise: Creating a New Reservation

Mr. Korsek called the hotel and gave you the following information regarding his stay:

- Check-in date: Feb 3, 2003

- Checkout date: Feb 4, 2003

- 1 adult, no children

- Rack Rate

Let's do this reservation:

- Click on **Reservations** icon on the main toolbar.

- Click on **New Reservation.**

- You will see the screen in Figure 26.

Figure 26: New Reservation Screen

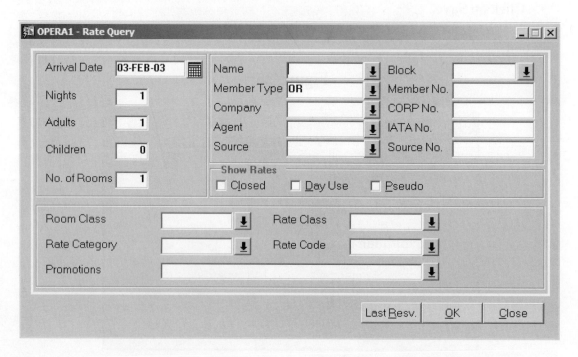

- Click on the calendar icon in the **Arrival Date** box.

- Choose Feb 3, 2003.

- Click on **OK.**

- Type "1" for Nights.

- Type "Korsek" in **Name** field.

- Press arrow next to **Name** field.

- You will see the screen in Figure 27.

Figure 27: Mr. Korsek's Profile Information Screen

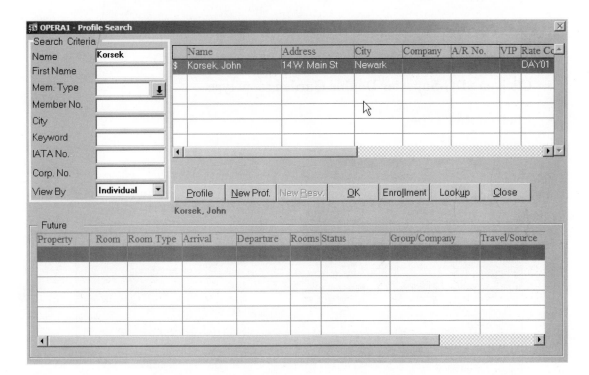

- Click on **OK.**

- You will see the screen in Figure 28.

Figure 28: Rate Code Selection Screen

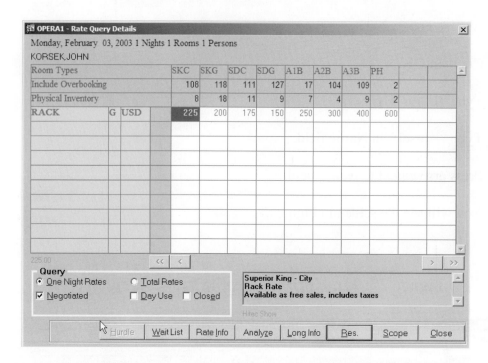

- Click on **SDG-Superior Double Garden** room type.

- Click on **Res. Type**

- You will see the screen in Figure 29.

Figure 29: Detailed Reservation Screen

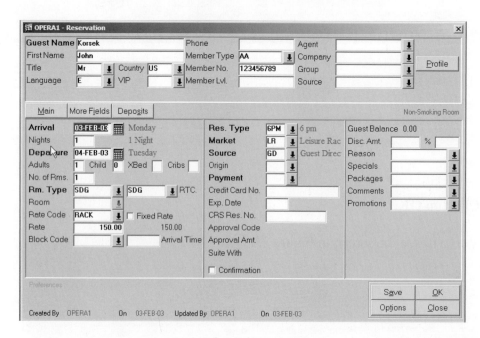

- Click on **Payment.**

- Click on **Visa Card.**

- You will see the screen in Figure 30.

- Click on the first credit card number (4444333322221111).

Figure 30: Credit Card Selection for Payment

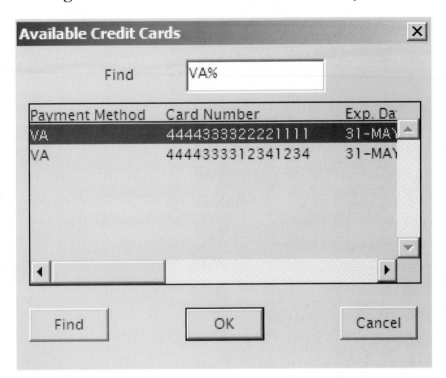

- Click on **Save.**

- You will get a confirmation code as in Figure 31.

- Click on **OK.**

- Click on **OK.**

Figure 31: Confirmation Code

The reservation is now made and saved in Opera.

Exercise: Check-in

Let's check-in one of the group guests who already has a reservation: Clay Booker

- Click on **Front Desk** icon on the main toolbar.

- Click on **Arrivals** on the side toolbar.

- You will see the screen in Figure 32.

Figure 32: Arrivals Screen

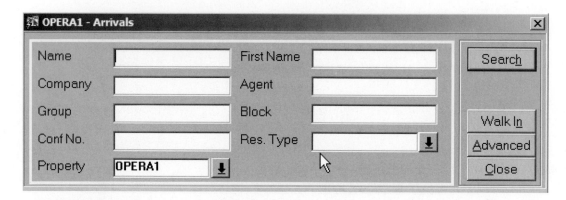

- Click on **Search.**

- You will see the screen in Figure 33.

Figure 33: Finding a Reservation in Check-in Process

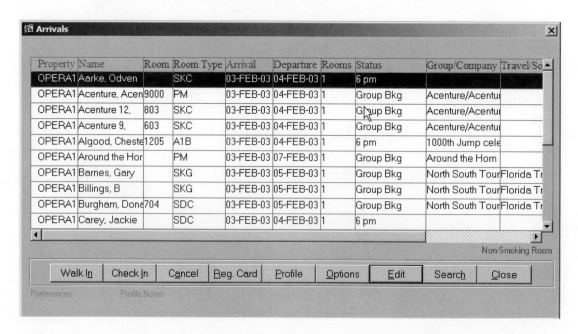

- Scroll down until you find **Booker, Clay.**

- Click on **Check-in.**

- You will see the screen in Figure 34.

- Mr. Booker is now checked in to Room 1505.

Figure 34: Check-in Message

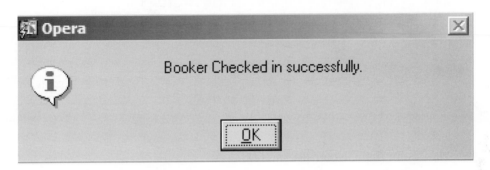

Exercise: Posting Transactions

Mr. Booker incurred the following expenses and charged them to his room. Record these transactions in *Opera*.

1. He had lunch in the restaurant. The food part of the bill was $20.00, and the beverage part of the bill was $5.00

   - Click on **Cashiering** from the main toolbar.

   - Click on **Billing** from the side toolbar.

   - You will see the screen in Figure 35.

Figure 35: Login Screen for Cashiering Functions

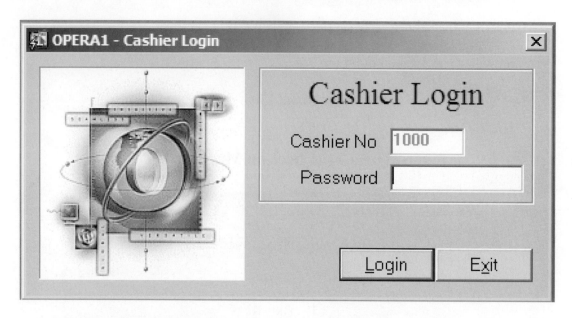

- Make sure that cashier no. is 1000.

- Type **OPERADEMO** for your password.

- Click on **Login.**

- You will see the screen in Figure 36.

Figure 36: Guest Search for Billing

- Scroll down until you see Room 1505 or Booker, Clay.

- Click on **Select.**

- You will see the screen in Figure 37.

Figure 37: Billing Screen

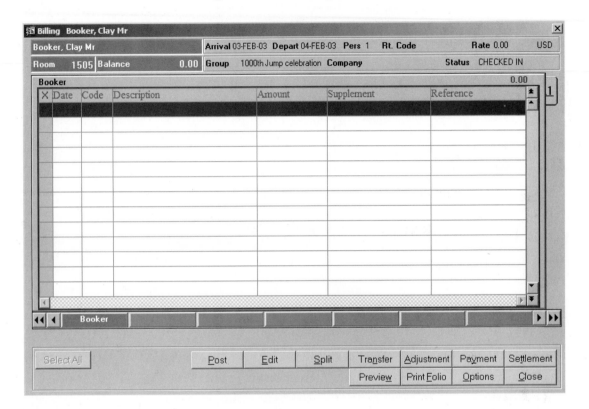

- Click on **Post.**

- You will see the screen in Figure 38.

Figure 38: Posting Screen

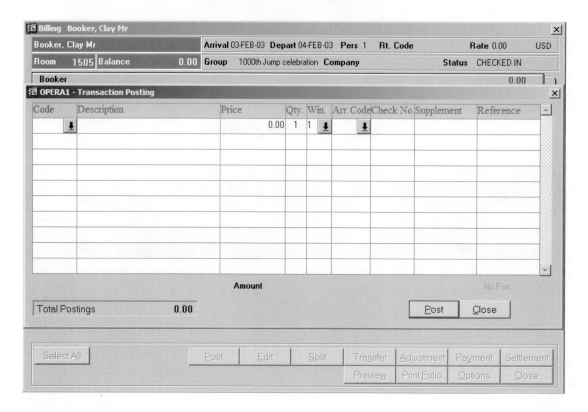

- Click on the arrow in the first column (Code).

- You will see the screen in Figure 39.

Figure 39: Transaction Codes Screen

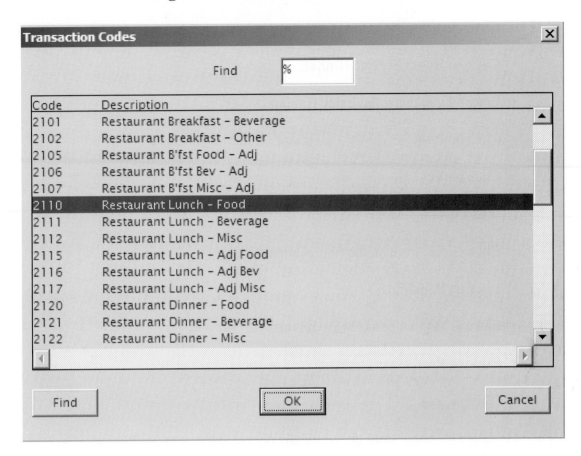

- Click on **Restaurant Lunch – Food.**

- Enter $20.00 under the **Price** column.

- Click on **Post.**

- Click on **Yes.**

- Click on the arrow in the first column (Code).

- Click on **Restaurant Lunch – Beverage.**

- Enter $5.00 under the **Price** column.

- Click on **Post.**

- Click on **Yes.**

2. Later in the day, he ordered dinner from room service. His bill was $45.00.

   - Click on the arrow in the first column (Code).

   - Click on **Room Service Dinner.**

   - Enter $45.00 under the **Price** column.

   - Click on **Post.**

   - Click on **Yes.**

3. He had a parking charge of $14.00.

   - Click on the arrow in the first column (Code).

   - Click on **Parking.**

   - Enter $14.00 under the **Price** column.

   - Click on **Post.**

   - Click on **Yes.**

4. He called his home from the hotel. His phone charge was $5.00.

   - Click on the arrow in the first column (Code).

   - Click on **Telephone.**

   - Enter $5.00 under the **Price** column.

   - Click on **Post.**

   - Click on **Yes.**

After all these charges, your transaction screen should look like Figure 40.

   - Click on **Close.**

Figure 40: Transaction Posting Screen after All Charges Being Posted

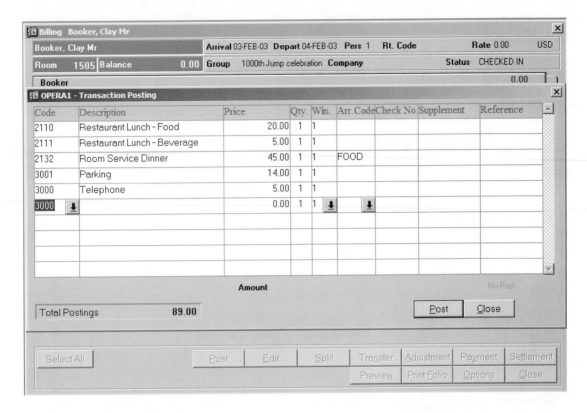

Exercise: Adjusting a Posting

You made a mistake in posting the parking charge for Mr. Booker. The actual charge was $10. Correct this mistake.

- Click on **Cashiering** from the main toolbar.

- Click on **Billing** from the side toolbar.

- Make sure that cashier no. is 1000.

- Type **OPERADEMO** for your password.

- Click on **Login.**

- Scroll down until you see Room 1505 or Booker, Clay.

- Click on **Select.**

- Click on **Parking Posting.**

- Click on **Edit.**

- Change the price to $10 from $14.

- Click on **OK.**

- Click on **Close.**

Exercise: Check-out

- Click on **Cashiering** from the main toolbar.

- Click on **Billing** from the side toolbar.

- Make sure that cashier no. is 1000.

- Type **OPERADEMO** for your password.

- Click on **Login.**

- Scroll down until you see Room 1505 or Booker, Clay.

- Click on **Select.**

- Click on **Settlement.**

- You will see the screen in Figure 41.

- Click on **Early Departure.**

Figure 41: Settlement Screen

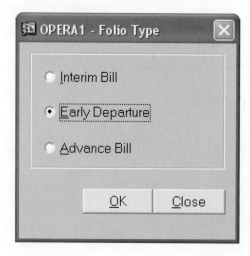

- You will see the screen in Figure 42.

- Make sure **Cash** is selected in **Payment Code.**

Figure 42: Payment Options

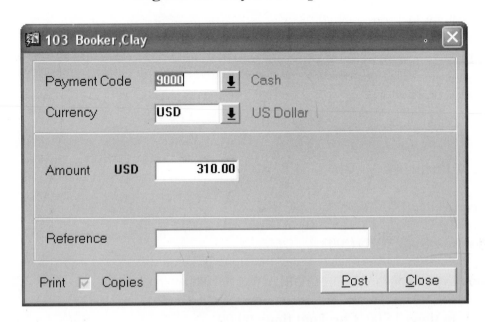

- Click on **Post.**

- Click on **Close.**

After you finish these exercises, remember to change the date of your computer back to its current date.

To change the date of your computer (for Windows 2000 and XP):

- Click on **Start.**

- Click on **Control Panel.**

- Click (or double click) on **Date and Time.**

- Change the date.

- Click **OK.**

Exercise #1   Use *Fidelio Opera* software to answer the following question.

John Jackson from Fahken Co. called the hotel directly and wanted to make a reservation. Use the following information and make his reservation.

Name: John Jackson

Address: 123 Main St., Stillwater, OK 74076

Phone: (312) 290 1212

Fax: (312) 290 1215

Date of Birth: 09/09/1971

Arrival Date: 03/09/2003

Departure Date: 03/11/2003

Room Type: Standard Double (DBL)

Check-in time: 15:00 **Checkout time:** 09:00

Mr. Jackson will need only one room, and he will stay in the room by himself. This will be a guaranteed reservation. He notified you that he wants to get a confirmation notice by fax.

Company Name: Fahken Co.

Address: 123 Central Blvd., Suite 190, Oklahoma City, OK 74945

Phone: (405) 234 5656

Fax: (405) 234 5657

Mr. Jackson is a member of your hotel's Executive Club. His membership number is as follows:

Executive Club Membership Number: 555666777

Expiration date: May 2005.

Mr. Jackson will pay by cash. You told him that he needs to deposit one night's rent in five days.

Mr. Jackson will pay his bill in US dollars. He would like to be included in the mailing list of New Rates (RAT).

You notified him that he will pay RACK rate (RACK RATE HB WALK IN), which is $150.00

Once you make the reservation, your manager notified you that he wants to be called when Mr. Jackson is checking out.

Exercise #2   Ms. Valerie Lake called the hotel directly and wanted to make a reservation. Use the following information and make her reservation. **Make sure to include your code with all transactions you make.**

Name: Valerie Lake

Address: 123 Fronan Street

State: Colorado   **Country:** USA.   **Zip/Postal Code:** 06790

Phone: +1 312 290 1212   **Fax:** +1 312 290 1215

Date of Birth: 09/09/1971

Arrival Date: 02/03/2003   **Departure Date:** 02/05/2003

Room Type: Double Room   **Check-in time:** 15:00   **Check-out time:** 09:00

Ms. Lake will need only one room and she will stay in the room by herself. This will be a guaranteed reservation. She notified you she wants a confirmation notice by letter.

Ms. Lake is a member of your hotel's Executive Club. Her membership number is as follows:

Executive Club Membership Number: 555666777

Expiration date: May 2005.

Ms. Lake will pay with a Visa credit card. Her credit card information is as follows:

Credit Card Type: Visa

Credit Card No: 4444 1111 2222 3333

Expiration Date: May 2005.

She would like to be included in the mailing list of New Rates.

You notified her that she will pay RACK rate.

Make sure that you send a fruit basket to her room on arrival.

Make the reservation. Note the reservation confirmation number.

She called you a week later and notified you that instead of 02/05/03 as her checkout date, she will check out on 02/06/03. Make this correction on her reservation.

Check in Ms. Lake. Please give her the room that *Opera* suggests.

After check-in, the minibar clerk has notified you that Ms. Lake consumed *two* beers and *two* sodas. The total cost for the minibar is $10. She also played tennis for one hour with a friend, and the rental cost for the tennis field per hour is $15. Ms. Lake also ordered a lunch from room service. The cost for the room service was $25. Post these transactions.

The morning of 02/05/2003, Ms. Lake receives an emergency phone call. She must return home. Please check Ms. Lake out early.

Section 4
Hotel Operational Audits

Using the Front Office Operational Audit as a Student

This section of *Hotel Operations Simulation and Auditing Manual* is an excellent tool for you to understand in a very practical way some of the day-to-day activities that go on in a hotel to manage guest services, information, and accounting. Your instructor may go over several of the various parts of the Front Office Operational Audit and the Housekeeping Operational Audit, that follow. And, they may even suggest that you use the packet as a guide in visits to hotel properties or internships in hotel properties to try to better understand them.

In using the audit as a classroom discussion exercise, you should be able to understand each question that is asked in the audit, and why it could be important. Because the audit is generic, that is, a large compilation of operational practices and considerations from many hotels of different sizes, types and affiliations, you should ask yourself which items would be important for a *particular* hotel that you or your instructor or group might choose.

If you are using the audit as a guide during a field visit to a hotel, go over it ahead of the visit and select some items from the audit that would be appropriate to disucss with the particular person you are visiting, such as the front office manager or the guest services manager or a receptionist or night auditor, for example.

If you are using the audit during an internship, review the items so that you select the ones that are consistent with the property where you are interning. Then use those items as a basis to observe and or interview the appropriate people in each department. The items represent a comprehensive view of the operations and responsibilities of the staff.

It is important to remember that parts of the operational audits will not apply to every hotel. Each property is different. The audits were designed to help hotel associates and managers to check on themselves to be sure they have all the right tools in place to service guests, care for associates, and make a profit.

What Is the Front Office Operational Audit?

Operational auditing is an organized review of a department's operating procedures. The *audit* presented here is the full version of what we (with Dr. Kathy Savage) presented in volume 12, number 6 of *The Bottomline* journal of the Association of Hospitality Accountants. We developed and field-tested a *Hotel Front Office Operational Audit* based on data collected from a series of hotel corporations. The result is a complete "audit questionnaire" that can be self-administered by hotel front office employees, hotel management, and internal or external auditors.

The management of most large hotel organizations and many smaller properties uses operational audits as part of their management control systems. One common approach to operational auditing is to use a detailed questionnaire to gather information about the efficiency and effectiveness of the organization. This article presents a comprehensive front office operational audit designed for full-service hotels. Its goals are to assist properties in quality improvement, training, and efficiency.

The Housekeeping Operational Audit

The Housekeeping Operational Audit can be used in the same way as the Front Office Audit. It was also developed based on work done by Mr. Don Wood of Oklahoma State University, soon to be published in an academic journal. This audit also used information from many large, full-service hotels and some limited-service properties, which were compiled, analyzed, and tested. The appropriate contacts in housekeeping would be the executive housekeeper, quality inspectors, supervisors and rooms division senior management.

Housekeeping is a fundamental support center in any hospitality establishment. In hotels, housekeeping generally employs the most people and has the highest costs of any department. Customer service, location, and facilities can bring in guests but without cleanliness, there will never be repeat guests or the ever-important positive word-of-mouth advertising. The functions of the housekeeping department are therefore essential but often taken for granted.

Through this operational audit, users have the opportunity to understand their housekeeping operations thoroughly and have their strengths and weaknesses noted for improvement. Using this operational audit will also have the indirect effect of boosting morale by showing employees the management's desire to listen, learn and improve. There are many benefits to conducting operational audits. To realize these benefits, requires the buy-in and commitment of senior management. Another key point is adequate follow-through and ongoing training after the execution of the audit. Although some questions in the following audit may seem to be duplicates, they are located in different areas of the audit and serve different purposes.

Note for Students

If your instructor has you use parts of the audit as a guide for a property visit or an interview, remember that not all hotels will use all the questions. In fact, the best way for you to use this would be to read it in advance and then just have a few of the most important questions summarized into one or two main questions that you could ask to "get the ball rolling" in the interview. Trying to go through the questionnaire, reading each question in an interview would be very tedious for all involved!

On the other hand, you may find that you are in a position to use either the entire questionnaire or parts of it as a project in a hotel. If that is the case, then be sure to involve the associates in its completion as suggested in the instructions that form the cover sheet of the audit itself.

Finally, if you are visiting a property, be aware of how important it is to be professional in demeanor and appearance. Make an appointment well in advance. Confirm it again before leaving for the property. And, make certain to dress professionally. All these will go a long way in showing how serious you are and how much you respect the hotel and the person you will be visiting. This, in turn, will gain you respect!

Hotel Management and the Operational Audits

How Can Hotels Use the Audits?

- The audits are comprehensive but flexible. They should address the needs of the particular local property. Hotel managers can carefully choose what parts they want to use; they can add and modify within categories as needed. The audits are only a guide. No one property would ever use every item in either of them.

- The supervisors and employees affected by the audit should be involved in the audit. The authors suggest that property management review the audit with the persons who conduct it. Management should be involved in conducting the audit themselves—especially *on* themselves in their own areas.

- The strength of the operational audit is in the follow-up phase. Employees should use the audit as a tool to follow up on items that needed attention. Used annually, the audit forces all concerned not to let things "slip" too far and prompts the user to set target dates for completing objectives that might come from the audit.

Conducting the Audit

The audit form offers a range of possibilities and uses. The flexibility of this tool comes from being able to modify the audit to fit the property. To accomplish this modification, the front office staff and other associated managers with the supervisors should review the items, deleting, modifying and adding as necessary. This will not all happen the first time around, but may be a successive, cumulative process as the property repeats the audit periodically.

If a lodging property has a quality assurance or continuous quality improvement program, the operational audit is a tool that should become an integral part of the program. The framework of the audit can help to keep quality teams and interdepartmental groups on target. It is a natural adjunct for one of these programs. Despite the presence of such programs, the hotel should conduct the Front Office Operational Audit at least twice a year. This provides a structure and timeline for intermediate and long-term projects.

After the initial review and modification to the document, the front office manager or appropriate department head should meet with employees or representatives from each shift that will participate. The front office manager should explain the purpose and process and answer questions. Indeed, it is much better if these shifts were involved in the audit process from the beginning. If they are involved from the beginning, employees will feel ownership of the audit and have an interest in the results. They will follow up on those items which require it – without close supervision and in collaboration with and support of supervisors and department heads.

Each affected shift and area should complete sections of the audit appropriate to them. Some sections are especially for supervisors and managers. When the audit is completed, supervisors and managers should meet with the employees or their representatives to review it. Identifying areas of strength is important so that management can reinforce and preserve these sections. Those involved can plan improvement strategies for those areas that need strengthening or modification. Attaching a timeline to correct deficiencies is important. This is necessary to follow up on the next audit. As designed, the audit form itself provides for automatic reminders on these items.

Some areas will surely remain the same in the audit and will require only a check mark. Nevertheless, they will at least have been considered. This is important in addressing changes in the environment, personnel, and markets.

If a hotel chooses not to use front-line employees to complete the audit, it becomes crucial to make certain that they understand why the hotel does the audit. Reviewing the results with the hourly associates is also important. The first time around, a property might want to employ an outsider (third-party agents) to plan and execute the audit. This person would bring the time necessary for this initial foray if time is a problem at the property. Nevertheless, these outside agents should involve all concerned.

Following are complete copies of the Front Office Operational Audit and the Housekeeping Operational Audit.

HOTEL FRONT OFFICE
OPERATIONAL AUDIT
Copyright © 1997

Patrick J. Moreo, EdD, CHA, Oklahoma State University
Gail Sammons, PhD, CHA, University of Nevada, Las Vegas

AUDIT QUESTIONS	Yes √	No √	NA √	COMMENTS/ Follow-up Action
PERSONNEL				
General				
Is there an orientation program?				
Does the front office manager identify training needs for the department?				
Is there an employee training program in place?				
Are training manuals available for each employee function?				
Are personnel cross-trained when not in conflict with union regulations?				
Are performance appraisals conducted on a timely basis?				
Are all guest comments concerning employees shared with the individual employee involved as well as supervisory personnel?				
Personnel Audit				
Are required posters and logs on hand?				
Are job descriptions maintained and updated on a regular basis?				
Are employee disciplinary procedures and house rules in compliance with company policies and procedures?				
Do employee awards/incentives programs occur on a regular basis?				
Are summaries of employee turnover analyzed?				
Are drivers of property vehicles properly screened and licensed?				
Scheduling				
Are written staffing guidelines for proper scheduling developed and followed?				
Are staffing levels adjusted and evaluated as needed?				
Is use of overtime analyzed?				
Is overtime scheduled?				
Are scheduling decisions reviewed by management?				
Organization Development				
If organization goals and mission statements exist, are they available to all employees?				
Are company policies communicated to departments and employees?				
Are staff meetings conducted on a timely basis?				
Are minutes of meetings communicated to employees when appropriate?				

AUDIT QUESTIONS	Yes √	No √	NA √	COMMENTS/ Follow-up Action
GUEST SERVICES				
General				
Does the front desk have proper signing so that guests don't wait in the wrong place?				
Are the procedures for guests waiting in lines for check-in/checkout frequently monitored and changed if necessary?				
Are procedures established for reception and processing of guests who are members of special hotel guest programs or who are destined for "special" (VIP, Club, Concierge, etc.) guest floors or sections?				
Are hotel guest service (restaurants, pool, etc.) hours known by front office staff?				
Are procedures established for processing guest mail?				
Are special procedures in place for processing guest express/special delivery mail?				
Are guest safety deposit box procedures established and implemented?				
Are affiliate (chain) current hotel directories available to the guests?				
Do front office receptionists and cashiers have friendly, positive attitudes?				
Telephone (PBX)				
Are phones answered promptly and courteously?				
Do telephone operators have full knowledge of hotel services as well as local services, attractions, and points of interest?				
Is an information directory maintained and accessible?				
Does the department provide for proper handling of messages taken for: guests in the hotel?				
guest with reservations?				
meeting rooms?				
rooms requesting no calls?				
In manual systems, are time stamps used on messages, phone charges, mail, and folios?				
In manual systems, are message lights turned off promptly?				
In automated systems, are unretrieved guest messages followed up periodically?				
Are procedures in place for wake-up calls?				
Are telephones for the hearing impaired available (in compliance with ADA audit): guest rooms?				
house phone?				
public phone?				
Do front office cashiers update local phone meters at checkout in semiautomatic systems?				
Are phone and operator service bills reviewed regularly for accuracy?				
Is credit received from telephone company for disputed calls?				

AUDIT QUESTIONS	Yes √	No √	NA √	COMMENTS/ Follow-up Action
GUEST SERVICES continued				
Telephone (PBX) continued				
Are equipment rental charges checked periodically?				
Are local and long-distance carriers reviewed regularly for quality, service, and pricing?				
In an automated system, is there a system for recording and reviewing phone charges for unoccupied or late checkout rooms?				

AUDIT QUESTIONS	Yes √	No √	NA √	COMMENTS/ Follow-up Action
GENERAL APPEARANCE				
General				
Is front entrance: kept clean and clear of trash?				
free of unnecessarily parked cars?				
fire lanes maintained at all times?				
Are lobby and public areas clean and in order and free of clutter?				
Is lighting inviting?				
Does the front desk have a "clean appearance", especially from the guest's perspective (e.g., free of disorderly and excessive credit card applications, signs, and brochures)?				
Are signs both necessary and appropriate to the setting?				
Is the hotel function board: appropriate to the setting, neat, and kept current?				
an assigned responsibility?				
Are concierge desk, bell stand, and other service areas attractive and neat in appearance (comfortable chairs, designer phone, fresh flowers, etc.)?				
Is storage of extra bell carts in a secured and out-of-sight area?				
Is the front desk set up for efficient operation?				
Staff				
Does someone monitor the appearance of staff periodically?				
Are all front office personnel: well groomed and neat?				
do they all have name tags and uniforms?				
do uniforms fit properly?				
Do front office staff present a professional image and appearance at all times?				

AUDIT QUESTIONS	Yes √	No √	NA √	COMMENTS/ Follow-up Action
GENERAL APPEARANCE continued				
Bell Staff				
Do bell persons offer a standard guest greeting at door?				
Do door/bell staff screen guests to direct them to the appropriate check-in area if necessary?				
Are cars and cabs greeted promptly?				
Does the bell staff smile and converse with the guest in a friendly manner?				
Does the bell person/door attendant present a professional appearance and professional conduct at all times, even when guests are not directly present?				
Do bell persons provide an orientation while rooming guest that ensures the guest is aware of all functions in the room as well as the services that the hotel has to offer?				
Does the bell staff "thank" the guest for his/her business?				
Can the bell staff give concise and accurate directions to local attractions and facilities?				
Are all service calls logged and timed, and is action time logged?				
Is the bell staff phone set up so that it can be answered at all times, even when someone is not present at bell desk?				
When a bell staff member is not available, is an alternate planned to provide service to the guest?				
Are valet and laundry delivered promptly when received?				
Is orientation and information about the hotel provided by van drivers when transporting guests?				
Are written tour handling procedures provided to the bell staff?				
Are guests pressured to use bell staff if not desired?				
Are all bell staff aware of proper procedures in checking and holding luggage?				
Is guest checked luggage in a secure area with claim checks issued accordingly?				
Is luggage to be sent to the guest's room properly labeled?				
Are procedures documented to move luggage to guest room, should guest wish to proceed to room without escort?				
Is the baggage storeroom clean and neat with luggage stacked neatly on the shelves?				
Is there a written procedure for handling claims of lost luggage?				

AUDIT QUESTIONS	Yes √	No √	NA √	COMMENTS/ Follow-up Action
GUEST AND ROOM STATUS MANAGEMENT				
General				
Is the front office bulletin or status board kept up-to-date?				
Does the front office manager review correspondence on a daily basis?				
Are front office employees required: to read all relevant memos?				
to initial all relevant memos?				
Is a memo binder kept up-to-date?				
Is a logbook used to monitor internal communication at the front desk?				
Is an end-of-shift checklist in use?				
Are there written procedures for front office employees in the event of equipment failure?				
Is there a control of inventories of paper supplies and other stock?				
If outside shoppers are used, are the results of past internal audits and reports reviewed in detail with all front office personnel?				
Are in-house files for folios and registration cards in good order with the facility to cross reference?				
Is a front office manual available to all front office, PBX employees and bell staff?				
Is the front office manual updated to reflect all current policies and procedures?				
In the manual system, do telephone operators receive guest information promptly?				
Is guest history information collected and used by the front office and other departments?				
Does the front office staff use the guests' names?				
Rooms Management				
Are procedures used to ensure that maximum revenue is realized on additional earnings from items such as late check outs, roll-aways, etc?				
Are procedures in place for maximizing multiple occupancy revenues?				
Are the names of all local front office and reservation managers in a current file?				
Are these individuals contacted regularly for overflow business and other formalities?				
Are there any recurring problems with daily room status controls and procedures? *(If so, note them in the comments column.)*				
Does the front office manager maintain control over out-of-order (off-market) rooms to ensure that they are returned for sale as soon as possible?				
Are room rates established in accordance with guidelines set by senior or corporate management?				

AUDIT QUESTIONS	Yes √	No √	NA √	COMMENTS/ Follow-up Action
GUEST AND ROOM STATUS MANAGEMENT continued				
Rooms Management continued				
Are rack rates adhered to? *(If not, comment on major reasons why.)*				
Are room rate variances reported and explained daily?				
Are airline and other major discounts managed in any special way on nights approaching full occupancy?				
Is there an established procedure for discounting parlor or other nondedicated sleeping rooms when they are used for sleeping?				
Is there a policy for selling suites and other high-priced units?				
Are procedures in place for processing cancellations and no-shows?				
Are procedures in place to ensure billing of guaranteed no-shows?				
Are reasons indicated for "DID NOT STAY" guests who left the hotel without completing their stay?				
Are registration cards that are marked "DID NOT STAY" reviewed by management?				
Are VIP, handicap, and other special request rooms blocked early in the day?				
On nights approaching full occupancy, are reservations checked for duplication periodically during the day?				
Is room availability assessed at regular intervals on nights the hotel is approaching full occupancy?				
On nights approaching full occupancy, are reservations assured by deposit or secured by guarantee blocked early enough in the day to ensure their availability?				
Is there a policy and procedure established for renting "special floor," handicapped, and other limited rooms at the front desk to prevent problems with a future block on those rooms?				
Guest Arrival				
Is there an adequate number of registration stations?				
Are special check-in procedures in place for processing group arrivals efficiently?				
Are front office employees knowledgeable concerning: acceptable credit cards?				
special promotion/packages/programs?				
special rates?				
special room types (e.g., nonsmoking, handicapped)?				
bed types in rooms?				
location of rooms?				
view from rooms?				
Are the explanations for codes, symbols, abbreviations, flags, etc. on both computer and manual parts of the front office readily available at each station?				

AUDIT QUESTIONS	Yes √	No √	NA √	COMMENTS/ Follow-up Action
GUEST AND ROOM STATUS MANAGEMENT continued				
Guest Arrival continued				
Are registration cards and folios complete including: guest signature?				
guest address?				
method of payment?				
ID, if necessary?				
time stamp, if necessary?				
At the time of check-in, do clerks verbally verify the: correctness and spelling of the guest name and address?				
room type?				
date of departure?				
Does the front desk staff inquire if the guest would like a bell person?				
Are procedures in place that allow early arrivals to be roomed as quickly as possible and accommodated on their other needs?				
Does the front desk staff offer guest directions to the room if a bell person is not used?				
Are the following procedures evaluated for guests who must be walked?				
Priority on categories of guests who will be walked?				
Compensations for inconvenience such as a complimentary night, discount, or gift?				
Apology letters from management for those guests who are walked?				
Are all walks recorded and analyzed?				
Are procedures and training established for handling "lost" reservations?				
Are guests preregistered as appropriate in both manual and computer systems?				
Does the front office staff maintain eye contact with guests?				
Are rooms and rates assigned in a manner that mutually maximizes room revenue and guest satisfaction?				
Are express or other special checkout services explained?				
Does the front office staff inform guests of the services the hotel offers, including revenue-generating areas such as restaurants and lounges?				
Does the front office staff adequately inform guests about features unique to the hotel such as the availability of continental breakfast, etc.?				
Does the front office staff double-check to ensure that they are giving guests the correct room key?				
Is a welcome packet used for key presentation at check-in?				
Is there a policy for upgrading to be done on a selective basis as marketing needs dictate?				
Does reservations and/or the sales department notify the front office well in advance on group blocks and booking pace?				
Is group information clarified and checked with the sales department prior to the group's arrival?				
Is a VIP arrival report prepared and reviewed by the front office staff?				
Are all concerned departments such as housekeeping, telephone, bell staff, and food and beverage informed of VIP and handicapped arrivals?				
Are automated check-in systems evaluated/reviewed on a timely basis?				

AUDIT QUESTIONS	Yes √	No √	NA √	COMMENTS/ Follow-up Action
GUEST AND ROOM STATUS MANAGEMENT continued			
Guest Departure			
Are expected checkouts flagged early in the day if the guest is scheduled to leave?				
Is there an adequate number of cashier stations?				
Is there an adequate number of automated checkout stations?				
Is there a drop box at the front desk for keys?				
Are all charges explained to the guest at the time of checkout?				
Is the guest thanked for his/her business?				
Are late checkouts processed properly?				
Are express checkout folios processed promptly?				
Are there special procedures in place to handle group checkouts or other large-volume checkout situations?				
Are automated checkout systems evaluated/reviewed on a timely basis?				
Key Control/Security			
Is a par stock of keys established and kept at the front desk?				
Is the number of keys in stock at the front desk sufficient?				
Are key inventories taken on a regular basis?				
Are key requisition records kept and reviewed?				
Is storage of guest room keys secured?				
Do front office personnel refrain from giving out guest room numbers?				
Is key control reviewed on a regular basis?				
Are key issues recorded?				
Are keys requested from the guest at checkout?				
Does housekeeping return keys to the front desk on a daily basis?				
Are manufacturers' security recommendations followed for all locking systems?				

AUDIT QUESTIONS	Yes √	No √	NA √	COMMENTS/ Follow-up Action
RESERVATIONS AND ROOM INVENTORY MANAGEMENT continued				
Reservation Procedures				
Is mail time stamped as it is received and processed?				
Are there adequate phone lines and staffing for incoming reservations?				
Is a room/rate availability board in the front office maintained and updated regularly?				
Is reservation correspondence filed by date and alphabetical order on a daily basis?				
Are rate cards, forms, and convention and house brochures available for guest correspondence?				
Are cancellation numbers provided for reservation cancellations?				
Is there a VIP list?				
Are there documented comp procedures for VIPs?				
Are VIPs and special requests blocked at time of reservation?				
Are same-day cancellations communicated between reservations and the front desk?				
Is there after-hours reservation coverage?				
If two reservation systems are used, are they compared for accuracy (e.g., internal reservations system and central reservations system)?				
Are confirmations sent on a timely basis and with a quality appearance?				
Are undeliverable confirmations so noted on the reservation for address accuracy?				
Are wait lists reviewed prior to opening up selling?				
For a manual reservation system: Is each reservation request recorded in a record of advance reservations, sometimes known as a tally book?				
Are cancellations or revisions subtracted and/or added to ensure that the tally book is always accurate?				
If reservation cards are used, are they filed by date of arrival and alphabetically?				
Do reservationists explain the types of reservations to potential guests: guarantees?				
advance deposit?				
unsecured?				
Travel Agents				
Are travel agent commissions paid promptly?				
Do you analyze travel agency commission expenses (monthly)?				
Do you review business generated by travel agents?				

AUDIT QUESTIONS	Yes √	No √	NA √	COMMENTS/ Follow-up Action
RESERVATIONS AND ROOM INVENTORY MANAGEMENT continued					
Rooms Inventory Control				
Is there a record of call conversion statistics?				
Do you set and review status controls and selling restrictions for rooms selling: minimum stays?				
closeout rate categories?				
Are rooms being sold in the most profitable order?				
Forecasting/Demand Analysis				
Do you research and analyze trends in the lodging industry?				
Do you conduct a local demand analysis of transient business?				
Do you compare demand to past years, months, weeks?				
Do you survey competition's rate structures on a regular basis?				
Do you accurately categorize and report occupancy, revenue, and average rate of each market segment, each night?				
Do you tabulate on a daily basis: no-show statistics?				
walk-in factors?				
early checkouts?				
Do you track accuracy of forecasts on a weekly/monthly basis, analyze discrepancies, and discuss strategies to improve?				
Does the reservations department contribute forecast information to: the annual budget?				
short-term forecasts?				
Are short-term forecasts prepared and distributed to operating departments: 10-day?				
3-day?				
Are there long-range forecasts?				
Group Rooms Control				
Is there a review of group rooming list due dates?				
Is there a review of incoming group pickup?				
Is there a review of group tentative room blocks beyond option dates?				

AUDIT QUESTIONS	Yes √	No √	NA √	COMMENTS/ Follow-up Action
GUEST LEDGER				
Credit				
Is a credit (limit) report maintained for each shift or each day?				
Are policies for guests who pay cash at check-in established and followed?				
Are policies for guests with advance deposits established and followed?				
Are check cashing and acceptance policies established and followed?				
Are direct billing procedures established and followed?				
Are clerks trained to be aware of potential skips and bad credit risks?				
Does a shift "bucket check" include a review of all imprinted credit card vouchers and authorization numbers?				
Are cashiers checking for late charges (breakfast, phone) at checkout?				
Guest Folios				
Are all corrections controlled and balanced?				
Are procedures established for the use of adjustments, allowances, discounts, and rebates?				
Does a company policy exist regarding adjustments to room revenue?				
Do the allowances indicate any specific problems with "sleepers" etc.?				
Is there a procedure for notifying management of total charges over a set limit to any one guest's folio?				
Are guest folio balances that are very small reported in the morning to the manager?				
Are tax-exempt rooms properly accounted for and listed on the tax exemption report?				
Are outside vendor charges to the guest ledger (such as valet) properly reconciled?				
Is there a procedure for allocation of package plans?				
Is a bucket to computer check done in computerized operations, if necessary?				
Foreign Money Exchange				
Are rates of exchange for foreign currencies updated on a daily basis?				
Are rates of exchange for foreign currencies provided to a guest exchanging moneys?				
Are the policies and procedures regarding exchange of foreign currencies evaluated on a regular basis to ensure service to the guest while maintaining cash security?				

AUDIT QUESTIONS	Yes √	No √	NA √	COMMENTS/ Follow-up Action
GUEST LEDGER continued				
Manual Operation Only				
Are continuation folios marked to and from for proper cross-referencing?				
Are all folios balanced?				
time stamped?				
current?				
and properly classified as guest ledger?				
Is a bucket check done nightly?				
Is bucket audited daily and master accounts transferred to City Ledger on a timely basis?				
Are alphabetical (registration cards) and numerical (folios by folio number) filing for departed guests done on a timely basis?				
Is security over all cash registers or cash drawers adequate?				
Are procedures for shift closing established and followed?				
Is there a review of cashiers reports?				
Do employees make cash drops on a timely basis, securing excess cash?				
Are deposit procedures in place and followed, including: witnessing and/or signing of sealed envelope?				
the transport of shift deposits to the drop safe?				
drop facilities constructed securely?				
Are there procedures for cash paid-outs (i.e., petty cash)?				
Do all paid-outs have proper documentation?				
Are cashier corrections, voids, and rebates documented and supported?				
Are all cash drawers kept locked, and is access controlled so that accountability is maintained? *(i.e., Is there only one person per cash drawer?)*				
If banks are transferred or used by more than one shift, are the banks counted before and after every shift?				
Are duplicate house bank keys and the combination to the general cashier safe properly secured?				
Is there a schedule or inventory of all house banks?				
Is the house bank balance reconciled to the general ledger?				
Are cash drawers and banks audited on a regular basis?				
Are records kept of the cash drawer and bank audits?				

AUDIT QUESTIONS	Yes √	No √	NA √	COMMENTS/ Follow-up Action
CITY LEDGER				
General				
Are procedures established for direct bill authorization?				
Is there a (manual or computer) direct bill authorization file of updated letters of authorization, with billing parameters defined?				
Are only authorized individuals permitted to sign direct billing accounts?				
Are past-due accounts reviewed periodically to determine adequacy documentation of collection efforts?				
Are City Ledger accounts receivable analyzed to determine: direct bills?				
sleepers?				
after departure (late) charges?				
prepaid accounts with charges?				
disputed accounts?				
delinquent accounts (over 60 days)?				
skips?				
tour vouchers?				
employee and intercompany accounts?				
and pay on departure accounts?				
Are procedures in place to properly age and act on various City Ledger categories?				
Is billing timely and in accordance with the established policy?				
Are turnaround times monitored for credit card receivable payments?				
Are procedures established and implemented for determining write-offs (e.g., sleepers or skippers)?				
Are accounting procedures implemented for trade outs, due bills, etc., and is the front office aware of them?				
Are procedures established for processing reservation no-shows guaranteed on credit cards through City Ledger billing?				
Are written efficient master account handling procedures in place and implemented?				
Are returned checks analyzed for propriety, aging, and immediately redeposited?				
Is a procedure established for the disposition of money received on accounts previously written off?				
Are credit card chargebacks reviewed on a timely basis?				

95

AUDIT QUESTIONS	Yes √	No √	NA √	COMMENTS/ Follow-up Action
CITY LEDGER continued				
Advance Deposits				
Are procedures established for receiving, recording and transferring of City Ledger advance deposit payments if they are handled through the City Ledger?				
Do group advance deposits shown in sales files and function book agree with posted folios?				
Are advance deposits recorded and logged by the reservations department by guest name and date of arrival?				
If manual folios are used, are the folios secured?				
Are advance deposit folios reconciled to either the general ledger or City Ledger?				
Upon guest check-in, are advance deposits properly transferred?				
Are revenues or refunds processed promptly on unused deposits?				

AUDIT QUESTIONS	Yes √	No √	NA √	COMMENTS/ Follow-up Action
CREDIT CARD USAGE				
Are floor limits for each type of credit card set and reviewed periodically?				
Do cashiers know the floor limits for credit cards?				
Are policies in writing for expired or unauthorized credit cards; do employees have knowledge of, and follow these policies?				
Is an explanation of credit card procedures offered to a guest during check-in?				
Are all credit cards authorized?				
Are all credit card vouchers complete with an authorization number, account number, clerk's initials, and folio numbers?				
Are credit card imprinters dated correctly?				
Are credit cards imprinted on both registration cards and vouchers?				

AUDIT QUESTIONS	Yes √	No √	NA √	COMMENTS/ Follow-up Action
EMERGENCY				
Is the first aid kit stocked?				
Are front office employees familiar with emergency procedures for: fire?				
bomb threat?				
power failure?				
terrorist attack?				
serious illness, death?				
hurricane or earthquake or other natural disaster?				
Are emergency evacuation routes established for all rooms, public areas, and back-of-the-house areas?				
Is there a procedure for identifying which rooms are occupied by handicapped guests so that assistance during evacuation can be provided?				
Is there a schedule for: checking fire extinguishers?				
monitoring alarm systems?				

AUDIT QUESTIONS	Yes √	No √	NA √	COMMENTS/ Follow-up Action
COMPUTERIZED FRONT OFFICE SYSTEMS **(This section is not meant to be comprehensive. These are sample questions regarding computerization.**				
Is a schedule followed for running computer backup reports and printing routine operation reports?				
Is there a list of computer equipment inventory?				
Are computer terminals logged off whenever users leave their stations?				
Have detailed computer "downtime" procedures been prepared, and do all front office personnel have access to these procedures?				
Are there adequate controls for: log-on codes?				
passwords?				
cashier codes?				
management keys?				
Are manuals maintained for all computer equipment and systems?				
Is the latest set of baseline programs properly labeled and kept in a secure location, easily accessible, but not in the computer room?				
Is an interface exception file printed and reviewed at least daily?				
Is there a maintenance program that ages and deletes history files?				

	YES	NO	NA	Comments/ Follow-up Action
TRAINING				
General/Operations				
Do you have:				
a housekeeping training manual?				
an employee training checklist?				
Do you have written procedures regarding:				
entering a guestroom?				
making a bed?				
cleaning guestrooms and public areas?				
personal safety?				
communicating with guests?				
training checklists?				
proper paperwork completion?				
daily pre-shift meetings?				
submitting and implementing employee ideas?				
key control?				
handling guest complaints?				
personal appearance standards?				
guest valet/dry cleaning?				
employee payroll?				
lost and found?				
telephone etiquette?				
quality assessment training?				
Do you have written safety training in the following areas:				
emptying waste containers?				
lifting?				
footwear to avoid slip/fall hazards?				
accident avoidance?				
turning mattresses?				
reporting injuries?				
mixing cleaning supplies?				
emergency numbers?				
Administration				
Do you have an Americans with Disabilities Act (ADA) training program that includes the following information:				
handicapped-accessible rooms and areas?				
signage for the blind or visually impaired?				
accommodations for guide dogs?				
telecommunication devices for the hearing impaired?				
job specifications, descriptions, requirements in compliance with ADA?				

	YES	NO	NA	Comments/ Follow-up Action
ORGANIZATION OF DEPARTMENT				
OrganizationChart				
Do you have a hotel organization chart?				
Do you have a department organization chart that delineates job functions?				
Teams				
Do you utilize guestroom attendant teams for:				
preventive maintenance?				
deep cleaning?				
special projects?				
Scheduling of Sections				
Do you have procedures in place and are followed to:				
utilize housekeeping reports to assign sections?				
monitor pay roll and productivity?				
prepare work schedules?				
Carts				
Do you have procedures in place and are followed to:				
stock GRA carts before shift?				
stock carts after shift?				
maintain cart supply par levels?				
perform preventative cart maintenance?				
Are cart supply par levels reviewed regularly?				
Storage				
Do you have procedures in place and are being followed to:				
store brooms, mops, buckets, cleaning material?				
store linen?				
store guest amenities and supplies?				
maintain cleanliness and organization of storage areas?				
secure storage area?				
Operations				
Do you have procedures in place to rush urgently required rooms?				
Do you have procedures in place to handle VIP guests?				
Do you have procedures in place to allow guests to enter while the room is being cleaned?				
Do you have procedures in place to follow up on maintenance issues?				
Do you have procedures in place to forward messages to GRA's?				
Do you have procedures in place to return unused room service items?				

	YES	NO	NA	Comments/ Follow-up Action
Operations continued				
Do you know the variable cost to clean a room:				
Do have procedures in place and are followed to:				
comply with DND signs?				
check deadbolt/electronic lock before knocking?				
enter a guest room?				
handle lost and found items?				
assure completion of room assignments?				
report problems to maintenance?				
report out-of-order rooms?				
complete housekeeping report?				
monitor service standards?				
have daily pre-shift meetings?				
guests refusing service?				
maintain security control?				
inspect guestrooms?				
inspect public areas?				
employee use of guest telephone or bathroom?				
turndown service?				
special guest requests?				
position GRA cart?				
COMMUNICATION				
Are procedures in place to ensure that the front desk is informed of clean rooms in a timely matter?				
Is there a telephone room status reporting system in place?				
Are procedures in place to bring back out-of-order rooms in a timely manner?				
Do you have procedures in place to contact managers and supervisors with guest complaints?				
Do you have a complaint management system?				
Do you have a complaint tracking system?				
Rooms Control in Housekeeping				
Do you have procedures in place and are followed to:				
call housekeeping office?				
report roomstatus?				
Interdepartmental **To the Front Office or Maintenance**				
Do you have procedures in place and are followed to report:				
ready rooms?				
problems to maintenance?				

	YES	NO	NA	Comments/ Follow-up Action
Interdepartmental continued ***To the Front Office or Maintenance***				
Do you have procedures in place and are followed to report:				
room status to front desk or logged into computer?				
out-of-order rooms?				
late checkouts?				
Do you have procedures in place and are being followed to:				
take phone messages?				
handle late checkouts?				
report ready rooms/checkouts?				
out-of-order rooms?				
Work Orders				
Do you have forms and are they used to report:				
room damage?				
defective equipment?				
maintenance requests?				
out-of-order rooms?				
Follow-Up				
Do you have procedures in place and are they followed to:				
pick up and log guest requests?				
recheck DND rooms?				
recheck amenities (i.e., towels)?				
Guests				
Do you have procedures in place and are they followed to:				
ensure telephone etiquette?				
use before entering a guestroom?				
use guest names?				
maintain standards during guest contact?				
use standard guest greetings?				
offer guest assistance?				
provide rapid response to guest requests?				
respond to guest complaints?				
verify guest intentions of checkout time?				
Employees				
Do you have procedures in place and are they followed for:				
employee meeting agendas?				
employee-to-employee relations and conduct?				
job safety?				

	YES	NO	NA	Comments/ Follow-up Action
CLEANING: ROOMS				
Are checklists available for use?				
Do you have procedures in place to give out and collect keys in a supervised and efficient manner?				
Do you use photos to teach proper room setup?				
Do you have procedures in place to ensure accurate time punching for employees?				
Entry				
Are procedures in place and being followed for:				
do not disturb signs (DND)?				
checking deadbolt/electronic lock before knocking?				
entering a guestroom?				
positioning the cart in the doorway?				
Bathroom				
Are procedures in place and being followed for cleaning the:				
vanity?				
mirror?				
rim, lid, bowl & base of commode?				
shower and curtain/door?				
floor?				
walls?				
towel rack?				
sink & fixtures?				
drains clean/clear?				
door?				
light switch plates?				
doorknobs?				
vent fan?				
bath tile?				
hair dryer?				
ashtrays?				
trash receptacles?				
soap dishes?				
glassware?				
ice bucket?				
coffee maker?				
towels stocked?				
follow up for replenishing towels to par?				
Living Area				
Are procedures in place and being followed to:				
open drapes upon entering room?				
vacuum the carpet?				
remove and return room service items?				
check carpet for spotting shampooing?				
check TV sound/picture/remote?				

	YES	NO	NA	Comments/ Follow-up Action
Are procedures in place and being followed to:				
set clock radio time/station/sound level?				
check smoke detector operation?				
arrange furniture?				
arrange/replenish collateral material?				
check hangers in closet?				
set heating ventilation and cooling (HVAC) controls?				
check and restock minibar?				
dust/clean:				
mirrors/pictures including tops and frames?				
lamps/shades?				
windows/sills?				
TV?				
telephone?				
clock/radio?				
furniture?				
refrigerator/wet bar?				
drapes/blinds/valance?				
closet shelf?				
iron/board?				
luggage rack?				
A/C vents?				
interior of dresser/armoire?				
walls?				
cobwebs/ceiling?				
smoke detector?				
all wiring/cables?				
ashtrays?				
Mattress and Bed				
Are procedures in place and being followed to:				
strip the bed?				
check condition of mattress pad?				
check condition of mattress and box springs?				
check condition of bedspread?				
rotate the mattress?				
check condition of new linen?				
make the bed?				
check cleanliness of bed skirt/base/under and behind bed?				
General				
Do you have a checklist for:				
guest room cleaning?				
guest amenities?				
amenity placement?				

	YES	NO	NA	Comments/ Follow-up Action
Do you have a checklist for:				
guest supplies?				
furniture placement?				
cart stocking?				
Are procedures in place and being followed for:				
start/end of day?				
VIP rooms?				
picking up daily room assignment?				
communication with guest in room?				
proper chemical use/handling?				
cleaning rag usage?				
deep cleaning schedule?				
changing room deodorizers?				
handling/disposal of hazardous materials?				
emergency odor problems?				
CLEANING: PUBLIC AREA				
Are checklists available for use?				
Corridors, Stairs, Elevators, and Vending Areas				
Are cleaning procedures in place and being followed for:				
vacuuming carpets?				
stairwell steps?				
handrails?				
ceiling?				
walls?				
baseboards?				
guest/service elevators?				
vending areas and vending machines?				
ice machines/drains?				
ash urns?				
trash receptacles?				
fire extinguisher boxes?				
windows/frames?				
doors?				
lightbulbs/fixtures?				
directional/emergency signs?				
Lobby				
Are cleaning procedures in place and being followed for:				
carpet?				
hard floor surfaces?				
walls?				
ceiling?				
baseboards?				
trash receptacles?				
public telephones?				

	YES	NO	NA	Comments/ Follow-up Action
Lobby continued				
Are cleaning procedures in place and being followed for:				
mirrors?				
furniture?				
chandelier?				
brass?				
marble?				
entry doors?				
windows?				
displays?				
signage?				
lighting fixtures?				
HVAC vents?				
planters?				
continental breakfast area?				
Restrooms				
Are cleaning procedures in place and being followed for:				
signage?				
door/frame/knob?				
sink?				
drains clean/clear?				
pipes underneath sink?				
vanity?				
mirrors?				
restocking soap dispenser?				
restocking hand towel dispenser?				
commode/urinal?				
partitions?				
restocking tissue dispensers?				
vending dispensers?				
floor?				
ceiling?				
walls?				
trash receptacles?				
HVAC vents/fans, odor control?				
Exterior				
Are cleaning procedures in place and being followed for:				
trash receptacles?				
ash urns?				
windows/frames?				
walkways?				
parking lot?				
delivery area?				
motor entrance?				

	YES	NO	NA	Comments/ Follow-up Action
Exterior continued				
Are cleaning procedures in place and being followed for:				
entry?				
pool area?				
pool furniture?				
light fixtures?				
signage?				
Back of the House				
Are cleaning procedures in place and being followed for:				
front desk area?				
offices?				
employee locker area?				
laundry?				
employee lounge area?				
restrooms?				
linen room?				
storage rooms?				
Food and Beverage Outlets				
Are cleaning procedures in place and being followed for food and beverage outlets and banquet facilities?				
General				
Are cleaning procedures in place and being followed for:				
houseperson duties?				
odor control in smoking sections of building?				
all building surfaces?				
recreation facilities?				
meeting rooms/suites/banquet facilities?				
GUEST SERVICES				
Do you have procedures in place and being followed for:				
lost and found articles?				
placing guest's personal items?				
VIP rooms?				
turndown service?				
special guest requests?				
breakfast door hanger requests?				
extra toiletry item request?				
roll-aways?				
wheelchairs?				
telephone etiquette?				
conversation with guest?				
baby beds?				

	YES	NO	NA	Comments/ Follow-up Action
Guest Services continued				
Do you have procedures in place and being followed for:				
concierge services?				
complete information on all property facilities?				
mini-bar restocking?				
EXPENSES				
Cost Control				
Do you have procedures in place and are being followed to:				
determine occupied rooms, dirty vacant rooms, rooms to be cleaned?				
breaking out the house?				
Budgeting				
Do you have procedures in place and are being followed to:				
utilize staffing guides?				
monitor productivity?				
monitor payroll?				
summarize capital improvement needs on a schedule?				
Quality Management				
Do you have procedures in place and are they being followed to ensure quality control according to set standards?				
Do you have quality assurance forms and are they being used?				
Inspections				
Do you have procedures in place and being followed to inspect:				
guest rooms?				
public areas?				
back-of-the-house areas?				
building condition?				
Age and Inventory Condition				
Do you have a system in place and is it being utilized to monitor age and condition of furniture, fixtures and equipment (FF&E)?				

	YES	NO	NA	Comments/ Follow-up Action
INVENTORIES				
How often are physical inventories taken?				
Do you have a known cost per amenity?				
Do you know the cost of the cleaning supplies?				
Are there procedures in place to require employees to sign for supplies?				
Are there procedures in place to monitor supply usage?				
Par Levels				
Do you maintain par levels for:				
linen?				
guest room amenities and supplies?				
cleaning supplies?				
Inventory Management				
Do you have procedures in place and or being followed to:				
maintain standards of guest room linen?				
stock GRA carts?				
inventory, store and issue all supplies?				
inventory, store and issue employee uniforms?				
Guest Room Amenities				
Do you have procedures in place and being followed to:				
check and replace guest room amenities?				
check and replace room collateral material?				
maintain specifications of guest room amenities?				
place amenities, collateral material and personal guest items in a designated location?				
PURCHASING				
Linen				
Do you have procedures in place and are being followed to purchase:				
linen by bid process?				
linen by specifications				
Guest Room Supplies and Amenities				
Do you have procedures in place and are being followed to purchase:				
guest room supplies by specifications?				
guest room supplies by bid process?				
Furniture, Fixtures & Equipment				
Do you have procedures in place and are being followed to purchase:				
furniture?				
carpet?				
TV/radio?				
drapes?				

	YES	NO	NA	Comments/ Follow-up Action
LAUNDRY				
In-House Linen Rotation				
Do you have procedures in place and are being followed to:				
record linen in/out?				
inventory linen?				
account for and dispose of unusable linen?				
clean bedspreads, blankets, and bed pads?				
handle food and beverage linen?				
Chemicals				
Do you have procedures in place and are being followed to:				
test water conditions?				
ensure proper wash formulas are used?				
pre-spot linens?				
inventory chemical supplies?				
proper chemical handling?				
Guest Laundry				
Do you have procedures in place and are being followed to:				
ensure garments are cleaned properly?				
inspect garments for damage prior to cleaning?				
replace buttons?				
do alterations/repairs?				
ensure proper garment tagging?				
contact guest immediately regarding damaged items?				
deliver items according to posted schedule?				
In-House Laundry				
Do you have procedures in place and are being followed to:				
treat stains?				
separate F & B linen?				
treat water quality if needed?				
weigh linen?				
adhere to wash formulas?				
Do you have procedures in place and are being followed to maintain:				
department safety?				
MSDS sheet?				
production log?				
pulling linen from carts?				
equipment?				
facility cleanliness?				
cleaning bedspreads, blankets and bed pads on a regularly scheduled basis?				
a linen discard log?				

	YES	NO	NA	Comments/ Follow-up Action
General Laundry				
Do you have procedures in place and are being followed to:				
train employees?				
use a duties checklist?				
PREVENTIVE MAINTENANCE				
Heating Ventilation and Cooling (HVAC)				
Do you have procedures in place and are being followed to:				
clean equipment?				
maintain a PM schedule?				
review PM on a timely basis?				
check/clean/replace filters?				
check coils?				
maintain HVAC checklist?				
Safety				
Are there procedures in place and are they being followed to:				
check smoke detectors?				
check all ceiling attached fixtures?				
ensure door peep hole is unobstructed?				
check condition of fire extinguisher boxes?				
Bathroom				
Are there procedures in place and are being followed to:				
test condition of water?				
check and maintain hair dryers and coffee makers?				
check bathtub/shower caulking bead?				
check floor tile?				
check operation of bathroom door?				
check flow of drains/shower-head?				
check operation of faucets?				
ensure all toilet fittings/seats are secure?				
toilet flushes and clears?				
test water temperature?				
Living Area				
Are there procedures in place and being followed to:				
check drapes/rods/hooks?				
ensure door threshold/frame is secure?				
check operation of TV/remote control?				
radio/stereo?				
telephone?				
ensure door locks/handles, security latches are working?				
all furniture is sturdy and maintained?				

	YES	NO	NA	Comments/ Follow-up Action
Living Area continued				
Are there procedures in place and being followed to:				
ensure minibar/refrigerator is working properly?				
ensure timely mattress rotation?				
check closet door operation?				
ensure carpets are deep cleaned on timely basis?				
check condition of all electrical cords?				
Interior Building				
Are there procedures in place and being followed to maintain:				
door, wall and ceiling finish?				
room attendant carts?				
corridor lighting?				
vacuums?				
banquet and meeting rooms?				
hotel entrance, lobby?				
health club facilities?				
Exterior Building				
Are there procedures in place and being followed to maintain:				
parking lot/curbing?				
landscaping?				
pool area?				
outdoor furnishings?				
signage?				
walkways?				
SAFETY/SECURITY				
Do you have a safety committee to actively promote safety issues?				
Do you have procedures in place to conduct security investigations?				
HAZCOM, MSDS and Blood-Borne Pathogens				
Are there procedures in place and being followed to:				
provide blood-borne pathogens training?				
provide employee safety equipment including:				
latex gloves?				
infectious waste liners?				
safety glasses with masks?				
protective clothing?				
Do you have OSHA hazardous communication posted?				
Do you have MSDS training?				
Are all chemicals properly labeled?				

	YES	NO	NA	Comments/ Follow-up Action
Do you have a safety committee to actively promote safety issues?				
Do you have procedures in place to conduct security investigations?				
Room Security/Safety				
Are there procedures in place and are being followed to:				
control keys?				
prevent unauthorized guest room access?				
report unsafe conditions?				
observe the (DND) do not disturb signs?				
Do you have emergency plan training?				
General				
Are there procedures in place and are being followed regarding:				
guest room inspections?				
accident avoidance training?				
fire/police procedures?				
emergency procedures checklist?				
first aid kit location?				
TECHNOLOGY				
Does your guest room phone system have remote messaging options?				
Do you utilize a computer to input guest room status?				
Do you utilize room scanners?				
Do you have separate computer lines in the guest rooms				
Does you hotel use PalmPilots or other handheld devices to manage room status? Are they wirelessly connected?				
Does your hotel use a telephone-based maintenance reporting system?				
Does your hotel use a computer-based scheduling system?				
Does your hotel have an internal communications network i.e., cell phones, pagers, or radios?				

Appendix
Forms for the Manual Night Audit Practice Set

These forms are to be used with the "Night Audit" exercise for University Inn found in Section 2.

Pearson Education, Inc.

YOU SHOULD CAREFULLY READ THE TERMS AND CONDITIONS BEFORE USING THE CD-ROM PACKAGE. USING THIS CD-ROM PACKAGE INDICATES YOUR ACCEPTANCE OF THESE TERMS AND CONDITIONS.

Pearson Education, Inc. provides this program and licenses its use. You assume responsibility for the selection of the program to achieve your intended results, and for the installation, use, and results obtained from the program. This license extends only to use of the program in the United States or countries in which the program is marketed by authorized distributors.

LICENSE GRANT

You hereby accept a nonexclusive, nontransferable, permanent license to install and use the program ON A SINGLE COMPUTER at any given time. You may copy the program solely for backup or archival purposes in support of your use of the program on the single computer. You may not modify, translate, disassemble, decompile, or reverse engineer the program, in whole or in part.

TERM

The License is effective until terminated. Pearson Education, Inc. reserves the right to terminate this License automatically if any provision of the License is violated. You may terminate the License at any time. To terminate this License, you must return the program, including documentation, along with a written warranty stating that all copies in your possession have been returned or destroyed.

LIMITED WARRANTY

THE PROGRAM IS PROVIDED "AS IS" WITHOUT WARRANTY OF ANY KIND, EITHER EXPRESSED OR IMPLIED, INCLUDING, BUT NOT LIMITED TO, THE IMPLIED WARRANTIES OR MERCHANTABILITY AND FITNESS FOR A PARTICULAR PURPOSE. THE ENTIRE RISK AS TO THE QUALITY AND PERFORMANCE OF THE PROGRAM IS WITH YOU. SHOULD THE PROGRAM PROVE DEFECTIVE, YOU (AND NOT PRENTICE-HALL, INC. OR ANY AUTHORIZED DEALER) ASSUME THE ENTIRE COST OF ALL NECESSARY SERVICING, REPAIR, OR CORRECTION. NO ORAL OR WRITTEN INFORMATION OR ADVICE GIVEN BY PRENTICE-HALL, INC., ITS DEALERS, DISTRIBUTORS, OR AGENTS SHALL CREATE A WARRANTY OR INCREASE THE SCOPE OF THIS WARRANTY.

SOME STATES DO NOT ALLOW THE EXCLUSION OF IMPLIED WARRANTIES, SO THE ABOVE EXCLUSION MAY NOT APPLY TO YOU. THIS WARRANTY GIVES YOU SPECIFIC LEGAL RIGHTS AND YOU MAY ALSO HAVE OTHER LEGAL RIGHTS THAT VARY FROM STATE TO STATE.

Pearson Education, Inc. does not warrant that the functions contained in the program will meet your requirements or that the operation of the program will be uninterrupted or error-free.

However, Pearson Education, Inc. warrants the diskette(s) or CD-ROM(s) on which the program is furnished to be free from defects in material and workmanship under normal use for a period of ninety (90) days from the date of delivery to you as evidenced by a copy of your receipt.

The program should not be relied on as the sole basis to solve a problem whose incorrect solution could result in injury to person or property. If the program is employed in such a manner, it is at the user's own risk and Pearson Education, Inc. explicitly disclaims all liability for such misuse.

LIMITATION OF REMEDIES

Pearson Education, Inc.'s entire liability and your exclusive remedy shall be:

1. the replacement of any diskette(s) or CD-ROM(s) not meeting Pearson Education, Inc.'s "LIMITED WARRANTY" and that is returned to Pearson Education, or

2. if Pearson Education is unable to deliver a replacement diskette(s) or CD-ROM(s) that is free of defects in materials or workmanship, you may terminate this agreement by returning the program.

IN NO EVENT WILL PRENTICE-HALL, INC. BE LIABLE TO YOU FOR ANY DAMAGES, INCLUDING ANY LOST PROFITS, LOST SAVINGS, OR OTHER INCIDENTAL OR CONSEQUENTIAL DAMAGES ARISING OUT OF THE USE OR INABILITY TO USE SUCH PROGRAM EVEN IF PRENTICE-HALL, INC. OR AN AUTHORIZED DISTRIBUTOR HAS BEEN ADVISED OF THE POSSIBILITY OF SUCH DAMAGES, OR FOR ANY CLAIM BY ANY OTHER PARTY.

SOME STATES DO NOT ALLOW FOR THE LIMITATION OR EXCLUSION OF LIABILITY FOR INCIDENTAL OR CONSEQUENTIAL DAMAGES, SO THE ABOVE LIMITATION OR EXCLUSION MAY NOT APPLY TO YOU.

GENERAL

You may not sublicense, assign, or transfer the license of the program. Any attempt to sublicense, assign or transfer any of the rights, duties, or obligations hereunder is void.

This Agreement will be governed by the laws of the State of New York.

Should you have any questions concerning this Agreement, you may contact Pearson Education, Inc. by writing to:

Director of New Media
Higher Education Division
Pearson Education, Inc.
One Lake Street
Upper Saddle River, NJ 07458

Should you have any questions concerning technical support, you may contact:

Product Support Department: Monday–Friday 8:00 A.M. –8:00 P.M. and Sunday 5:00 P.M.-12:00 A.M. (All times listed are Eastern). 1-800-677-6337

You can also get support by filling out the web form located at http://247.prenhall.com

YOU ACKNOWLEDGE THAT YOU HAVE READ THIS AGREEMENT, UNDERSTAND IT, AND AGREE TO BE BOUND BY ITS TERMS AND CONDITIONS. YOU FURTHER AGREE THAT IT IS THE COMPLETE AND EXCLUSIVE STATEMENT OF THE AGREEMENT BETWEEN US THAT SUPERSEDES ANY PROPOSAL OR PRIOR AGREEMENT, ORAL OR WRITTEN, AND ANY OTHER COMMUNICATIONS BETWEEN US RELATING TO THE SUBJECT MATTER OF THIS AGREEMENT.